Ferret Breeding

Other books by James McKay published by Swan Hill Press

Complete Guide to Ferrets

The Complete Jack Russell

Ferret Breeding

A Modern Scientific Approach

JAMES McKAY

Director
The National Ferret School

SWAN·HILL
PRESS

DEDICATION

To Jane and Tom, my heroes, and my best friends,
for your never ending help, encouragement,
enthusiasm and support.

First published in the UK in 2006
by Swan Hill Press, an imprint of Quiller Publishing Ltd

British Library Cataloguing-in-Publication Data
A catalogue record for this book
is available from the British Library

ISBN 1 904057 56 X
    978 1 904057 56 7

Typeset by Phoenix Typesetting, Auldgirth, Dumfriesshire
Printed in England by Henry Ling Limited, at the Dorset Press, Dorchester, DT1 1HD

Swan Hill Press

An imprint of Quiller Publishing Ltd
Wykey House, Wykey, Shrewsbury, SY4 1JA
Tel: 01939 261616 Fax: 01939 261606
E-mail: info@quillerbooks.com
Website: www.countrybooksdirect.com

CONTENTS

INTRODUCTION

Ferrets are fascinating animals that are immensely popular throughout the world. Large numbers of people keep ferrets, and for many reasons – as pets, working companions, fancy/exhibition animals and, often, simply because they find ferrets so interesting. Ferrets are also bred for, and extensively used in, medical research.

The aim of this book is to help breeders produce better ferrets, and ones that meet the criteria to help the animal achieve success in its designated role. The book is not intended to encourage people to breed, indiscriminately, large numbers of ferrets, which will then, inevitably, end their lives at one of the many 'ferret rescue' centres or refuges; or even worse, be abandoned in fields and towns. Such action is immoral, and I have no qualms about condemning all such actions.

I sincerely believe that breeders of *all* species should have an ethical approach, and would recommend that every club, society and other organisation involved with the breeding of animals, should adopt and enforce a code of ethical practice, such as the one featured in this book (Appendix 5).

Before embarking on any breeding programme – no matter how small or seemingly unimportant – owners should ask themselves *why*. If you cannot convince yourself that there is good reason to breed ferrets – *don't*.

Why do ferret breeders need to know about anatomy and physiology etc? While it is true that it is possible to breed ferrets without detailed knowledge of the workings of the ferret's body, such knowledge is essential if one is to be able to get the best results from a breeding programme. Also, if (or maybe that should be 'when') a problem occurs within the breeding programme, or one of the ferrets becomes ill, knowledge of the ferret's anatomy and physiology can help pinpoint and even solve the problem.

Why genetics? Many breeders fight shy of genetics, believing that it is far too complicated a subject for them, and also believing that it is not necessary to have knowledge of genetics in order to breed good ferrets. As with anatomy and physiology, this is true to a degree, but a good working knowledge of the main principles of genetics will prove indispensable to any breeder who wishes to run a breeding programme that will improve the ferrets, generation after generation. As this should be the main reason for anyone to breed ferrets, it should also be seen that a thorough understanding and working knowledge of genetics is essential to responsible ferret breeders.

We have a major problem when dealing with the genetics of the ferret; no published genetic research has ever been carried out on the species, a shocking but unfortunately true state of affairs. This means that, in this book, I have had to concentrate on the basics and generalities of genetics, without being able to give many definitive statements on ferrets specifically. While some would say this is a cop-out, it should be remembered that all life – animal and plant – is based on DNA, and the laws of genetics apply equally to all species. Therefore, the principles outlined in this book are totally valid and applicable to the ferret. In order to guide the reader, and show genetics in action, it has been necessary to give examples of the breeding of different varieties of several species; again, the principles are the same in all species, and so the reader should be able to extrapolate the information relevant to the ferret. Likewise, this book will also look at, explain and advise on different breeding methods, such as in-breeding, line-breeding, and out-crossing, giving both the positives and the negatives of all methods.

In the production of this book, I have received much assistance, guidance and support. In particular, I would like to express my sincere gratitude to my wife, Jane, and my son, Tom. Despite a huge workload, my wife and son have helped and supported my writing efforts, making many sacrifices along the way, missing family days out and seeing me disappear into my office early in the morning, in the evening, and for many hours in the night. They have both had to endure my obsession with getting it right – even when this meant that I had to re-write large parts of my manuscript, and re-take photographs. Throughout this time, they have kept smiling, and always gave me encouraging words – not to mention lots of hot cups of coffee. Thanks to the both of you. I hope you feel this, the finished object, was worth all the time and effort that we have expended on it. This was another team effort that has seen us win through.

I must also thank my good friend, and excellent veterinary surgeon, Ryan James MRCVS. Ryan painstakingly read through all of the manuscript, recommending alterations and amendments, and pointing out my mistakes. At times, my demands upon Ryan's time were far too much but, on every occasion, with a smiling face and great humour, he played his role to the full. Thank you.

Last, but by no means least, I must thank my publisher, Andrew Johnston. When he commissioned me for this book, Andrew rightly set deadlines which, due to a whole heap of mishaps on my part, went sailing past without the appearance of the manuscript. Andrew has been helpful, understanding and extremely patient throughout this trying time. Again, I hope the finished book proves that Andrew was right to have such faith in my abilities.

Obviously, any mistakes within the covers of this book are mine.

James McKay
Derbyshire

CHAPTER ONE

INTRODUCTION TO FERRETS

What is a Ferret?

This seemingly simple question does not, unfortunately, have an easy answer, as even the 'experts' cannot agree. If, as many believe, the ferret is a domesticated animal that was once wild, when, why and where was it domesticated? It is true to say that there are many theories put forward as to the origins of the ferret, and each has its adherents.

The first historical mention of the ferret is in the Bible. In Chapter 11 of *Leviticus*, the ferret is listed as one of the animals that God forbade us to eat. However, in some versions of the Bible, the same word is translated as weasel or even lizard, so this reference is obviously controversial. Some people ask how the same word can be translated differently; language changes and evolves, and many words have done so in my time.

The Greek playwright Aristophanes mentions the ferret in his comedy *The Acharnians* (*circa* 450 BC) and the Greek philosopher Aristotle lists the ferret in his *Historia Animalium* (*circa* 320 BC). However, these references too are considered to be somewhat controversial, as scholars disagree on the correct translation from the Greek.

The first universally accepted reference to the ferret is that by Strabo, a Greek historian and geographer. In his book *Geographica* (*circa* AD 20), Strabo writes of an animal that was said to have been bred in captivity in Libya, and used by the native peoples for hunting rabbits. Strabo states that the animal was used to bolt the rabbits from their underground burrows. If bolting was not achieved, then the animal would hang on to the rabbit while it was dragged out on the end of its lead, complete with rabbit. Strabo claimed that this animal was fastened on a line and always muzzled, and so it held its quarry in its claws while being dragged out on the line. Today, members of the Ruafa tribe, in Morocco, still hunt rabbits employing the services of a muzzled ferret-like animal.

Carolus Linnaeus, the Swedish naturalist and physician who, among many other achievements, was responsible for developing a system of classification of all living things (first published in his botanical work *Systema Naturae*, in 1758), and known as the father of taxonomy, also seems to give credence to this reference by Strabo, as he listed the locality of the species he named *Mustela putorius* as Africa. However, neither of the animals from which most scientists believe the ferret to be descended (the European polecat – *Mustela putorius* – and the Steppe polecat – *Mustela eversmanni*) come from Africa.

Some authorities state that the ferret is always white with red eyes (Linnaeus described the eyes as 'rubicund'), and that the animal must be kept in a warm environment to prevent it dying from exposure. Owing to its tender and delicate disposition, it has also been stated that, if they escape, the ferrets will be dead within 48 hours. The polecat, argue these people, is an entirely different animal, as it can withstand cold and is never white, and this proves that the ferret's ancestors originated from the southern hemisphere.

Readers of this book will know that these statements about the ferret are untrue; ferrets can withstand the cold very well, and the animal is bred in many colours and hues, from an almost exact replica of the European polecat, to pure white, and every shade in between. Recently, in the UK, researchers endeavoured to find true polecats, and had great difficulty in distinguishing these animals from feral ferrets, or even ferret/polecat hybrids, such are the similarities between these two animals.

Ferrets *can* live in the wild, when they are known as feral. Feral colonies of ferrets are to be found in almost every country throughout the world; in the UK, the Island of Mull (in the Inner Hebrides) has a strong colony of feral ferrets, while in New Zealand, where ferrets were deliberately introduced by European settlers from 1882, the ferrets have become a danger to the native fauna, and have driven at least one species – the kiwi (*Apteryx spp*), the national emblem of New Zealand – to the verge of extinction.

The name 'ferret' comes from the Latin *furonem*, which means thief (hence the word *furo*, the third part of the ferret's Latin name, when one is using the trinomial system of naming animals). Today, 'ferret' is also used in the English language as a verb, meaning to search diligently, to remove from a hiding place, or to draw out by shrewd questioning. Other names for the ferret and its wild relatives include fitch, fitchet, poley, stinkmart, stinkmarten, foulmart, foulmarten, foumart, fulimart; most of these names originate from the smell of the ferret. Poley and polecat ferret were terms originally use to describe a hybrid of the wild polecat and its domesticated cousin, the ferret. Today, however, the terms are used erroneously and misleadingly, to describe any ferret that has polecat markings, which should more accurately be known as fitches or fitchets.

There are many legends about ferret/polecat hybrids here in the UK, where many ferreters claim to have true polecats. The provenance of these animals often leaves much to be desired, and many such 'polecats' are simply dark fitch ferrets. The vast majority of those who claim to have hybridised a ferret and a polecat, claim that the offspring of the union are first-class rabbiting ferrets, and yet the truth is the opposite. Man has worked diligently to remove the unwanted elements of a polecat's behaviour, for thousands of years, and from the polecat produced the ferret. What, then, can be the benefit of re-inventing the wheel, and putting polecat genes that have been selectively bred out, into the domestic ferret's gene pool? My own experience of polecat/ferret hybrids is that they are beautiful-looking animals that are extremely skittish, and thus entirely unsuitable for working.

There are many historical references to ferrets and their uses, and I would point interested readers to one of my other books *The Complete Guide to Ferrets* (Swan Hill Press, 1994), and other books listed in the Bibliography.

The Ferret's Relatives

The ferret belongs to the Mustelidae, or weasel tribe, and is closely related to such animals as the otter, the badger and the skunk; it is an obligate carnivore. The Mustelidae is a diverse family of mammals that includes terrestrial, arboreal and aquatic species. While most are true carnivores, some species have evolved very specialised feeding. There are twenty-six genera, sixty-seven species and over four hundred subspecies of mustelids recognised by scientists to date. Mustelids naturally occur throughout the world, with the exception of Antarctica, Australia, Madagascar, New Guinea,

New Zealand, most of the Philippines, Sulawesi, the West Indies, and most oceanic islands, although feral and/or introduced populations are now in some of these places.

Almost without exception, mustelids are renowned for their fur, and many species suffered because of the fur trade, while many continue to be of economic significance in some communities. The best illustration is the sable (*Martes zibellina*), which was extensively hunted for its pelt until fairly recently; the species is now farmed.

There are five subfamilies within the Mustelidae, *viz*; *Mustelinae* (weasels), *Mellivorinae* (honey badger or ratel), *Melinae* (badgers), *Mephitinae* (skunks) and the *Lutrinae* (otters). The pelage is either uniformly coloured, striped or spotted, and some species turn white in winter in the northern parts of their range (a phenomenon controlled by photoperiod). In most species, the body is long and slender; however, the wolverine and badger are stocky. All have short ears, which are either rounded or pointed, and have short limbs with five digits on each. The claws are non-retractable, and are curved and compressed, with the badger's claws being larger and heavier, as an adaptation for digging. In otters, the digits are usually webbed.

Males of all species in this family have a baculum (a bone in the penis), and most species have well-developed anal scent glands. Skulls are sturdy, with short facial regions, and the dental formula is:

(i 3/2 - 3, c 1/1, pm 2 - 4/2 - 4 , m 1/1 - 2) x 2 = 28 – 38
(*Enhydra* is the sole genus with two lower incisors.)
(See Page 34 for an explanation of its dental formula)

All mustelids are either nocturnal or diurnal, sheltering in trees, burrows or crevices, while badgers usually dig elaborate burrows, known as setts. The smaller, slender forms in this family move with a characteristic undulating, wave-like motion and, when excited, bounce with stiff legs. The larger members of the family move with a rolling bear-like shuffle.

Mustelids are mainly carnivorous (otters eat mainly aquatic animals), although some species occasionally feed on plant material, while a few are omnivorous. All have highly developed hearing and some species have good sight, but all tend to hunt by scent, and many species, including *Mustela, Poecilogale, Gulo*, and certain badgers, are storers and hoarders of food. Many mustelids have anal glands capable of producing a fetid secretion when threatened or attacked.

Delayed implantation occurs in many species of this family (but not the ferret). Although gestation in mustelids is between thirty-five to sixty-five days, in *Lutra canadensis* (the river otter), pregnancy can last as long as twelve months.

There is usually a single litter each year, although some species will produce a second litter if mated early in the summer, and multiple litters can be produced in captive animals, by manipulation of the photoperiod. Offspring are self sufficient at about eight weeks, sexually mature between one and two years, and can live five to twenty-five years.

Classification of the Mustelidae

ORDER CARNIVORA – 7 FAMILIES, 93 GENERA, 231 SPECIES
This order includes felids (cats), canids (dogs), bears (including polar and grizzly), racoons (including coatis and giant pandas), weasels (including stoats and polecats), civets (including meerkats and mongooses) and hyenas.

FAMILY MUSTELIDAE – 26 GENERA, 67 SPECIES
Mustelidae are to be found all over the world, naturally occurring in every continent except Australia and Antarctica. Their habitat ranges from arctic tundra to tropical rainforest on land, in trees, in rivers and in the ocean. Animals in this tribe range in size from the diminutive least weasel (*Mustela nivalis rixosa*), which measures 150 mm (6in) head to tail with a tail length of 30–40 mm (1¼-1¾in), weighs as little as 30 g (just over 1oz) and is the smallest carnivore known to man, to the enormous grison (*Galictis vittata*), a mammal from Central and South America, which resembles a wolverine and can attain sizes of up to 1200 mm (48in) head to tail with a tail of up to 650 mm (26in) and weighs in at up to 30 kg (66lb). One of the most recently described subspecies of the Mustelidae, is the Hainan small-toothed ferret-badger (*Melogale moschata hainanensis*).

SUBFAMILY MUSTELINAE – 10 GENERA, 34 SPECIES
These include the grisons, martens, mink, polecats and weasels. They are terrestrial hunters of small vertebrates, although some (particularly the martens) are excellent climbers.

Members of the Subfamily Mustelinae

M. africana	the tropical weasel
M. altaica	the mountain weasel
M. ermininea	the common stoat (ermine)
M. eversmanni	the Steppe polecat
M. felipei	the Columbian weasel
M. frenata	the long-tailed weasel
M. kathiah	the yellow-bellied weasel
M. lutreola	the European mink
M. lutreolina	the Indonesian mountain weasel
M. nigripes	the black-footed ferret
M. nivalis	the European common weasel
M. nivalis rixosa	the least weasel
M. nudipes	the Malaysian weasel
M. putorius	the European polecat
M. putorius furo	the domesticated ferret
M. sibirica	the Siberian weasel
M. strigidorsa	the back striped weasel
M. vison	the American mink
Vormela peregusna	the marbled polecat
Martes americana	the American marten
M. flavigula	the yellow-throated marten
M. foina	the beech marten
M. martes	the pine marten
M. melampus	the Japanese marten
M. pennanti	the fisher
M. zibellina	the sable
Eira barbata	the tayra
Galictis cuja	the little grison
G. vittata	the greater grison
Lyncodon patagonicus	the Patagonian weasel
Ictonyx striatus	the Zorilla, or striped polecat
Poecilictis libyca	the Saharan striped weasel
Poecilogale albinucha	the white-naped weasel
Gulo	the wolverine

Modern Uses for Ferrets

Until fairly recently in their history, ferrets have been used for one thing – hunting. In the nineteenth century, ferrets were employed by *ferret meisters* in Germany and Holland, to control the rats and other rodent pests around granaries. The first ferrets imported into the United States were taken by these ferret meisters, to do the same work in the New World. The American Massachusetts Colonial Navy employed ferrets on board their ships for the same reason, to control the rats. In the UK, ferrets have long been used for rabbit and rat control, and still are.

However, in about 1970, ferrets became popular in many countries as pets and also as fancy animals (animals to be exhibited). The popularity of ferrets as pets has boomed in many countries, especially the United States and the UK, although no one seems to be able to quantify this popularity. In the United States, ferrets are ranked as the third most popular pet, behind cats and dogs, and command very high prices in comparison with the prices of ferrets in the UK – in some cases prices in the United States are more than a hundred times higher than in the UK.

In the 1970s, in the UK, a new sport was formed – ferret racing. Today, ferret racing events feature strongly at many country fairs and similar events throughout the country and the author also conducts ferret races for charities. When properly organised, the crowds find the spectacle of ferret racing fascinating, and even the ferrets seem to enjoy themselves, while the charities concerned raise large amounts of cash for their chosen cause.

The legend surrounding the invention of this sport is that oil workers (in the United States) used ferrets to pass lines through the newly laid and welded pipelines; once through, the lines would be attached to cameras, which would be hauled through the pipes to help check the quality of the welds. At night, after the day's work was done, and with very little for the workers to do, they would take bets on the fastest ferret to go through a length of pipe.

When the idea arrived in the UK, it was suitably tweaked to allow for British conditions. Today, the average ferret race takes place between four to six ferrets, which have to run down identical lengths of piping (all of the same bore). At intervals along the pipes, gaps are left (to help the public see where the ferrets are), and the trick is to encourage the ferret to ignore them and continue to the end of the piping, without physically interfering with the ferrets and/or the tubing. While some ferret owners take such sport very seriously, and strive to breed the ideal racing ferret, most see the events as light-hearted fun and entertainment.

Ferrets have been – and continue to be – used in industry, for threading cables and similar objects through pipes and confined spaces. They were used to help lay the camera cables for the wedding of HRH the Prince of Wales and Lady Diana Spencer. Ferrets were also used to lay cables for several millennium celebrations in the UK.

As well as high-profile tasks such as these, there are many owners of small businesses who use the ferrets for similar tasks. Many burglar alarm fitters and electricians use ferrets to pass cables and wires under floorboards, without the need to rip up the flooring in houses, offices and factories, while farmers use ferrets to help them locate blockages in field drains. Without the use of the ferrets, the farmers would have to dig up the whole field to find and repair the blockage in the drains. To do this work the ferret is equipped with a small transmitter, usually carried around the ferret's neck on a collar. This collar gives out a signal, which is picked up on a hand-held reliever carried by the farmer or his staff. When the ferret gets to the blockage, the animal obviously has to come to a halt, and will eventually turn back; the farmer marks the spot where the ferret turned, and then enters a ferret from the other end of the drain, again marking the area where the ferret cannot get through. The blocked area is then clearly marked, and the bulldozers can do their job, thus saving large expenses that would have been necessary without the use of the humble ferret.

Ferrets are also used in bio-medical research. Today, ferrets are used for research into a cure for human influenza, a malady that can also badly affect ferrets naturally. Influenza vaccines, such as are administered to aged, young and infirm humans, are produced from work on ferrets. The ferret is also used as a laboratory (research) animal for physiology, virology, immunology, pharmacology, toxicology and teratology. While some of these laboratory uses are for the benefit of humans, it should also be noted that many are for the direct benefit of ferrets and other animals kept as pets.

CHAPTER TWO

BASIC ANATOMY AND PHYSIOLOGY

In order to be able to breed any species effectively and efficiently, the breeder must have a working knowledge of that species's anatomy and physiology. In order to be able to ascertain what has gone wrong – and correct it – one must know what happens when everything goes right. It should be the aim of every breeder to improve the animals within the breeding programme at every breeding. It should also be the aim (even if not the achievement) of all breeding programmes to obtain a 100 per cent success rate, i.e. all offspring should live to at least weaning age.

The following outlines the main systems of the ferret that affect the breeding of the animal; some items (such as sight etc.) are not covered here.

The Body's Cavities

The mammalian body has three cavities:

- The thorax
- The abdomen
- The pericardium

All three of the body's cavities are lined with serous endothelium, which is a shiny, smooth membrane that produces a lubricant between two surfaces.

The thoracic cavity is lined with pleura, a serous membrane, and is divided into two pleural cavities. A mammal's lungs are in pouches in the pleura, i.e. each of the lungs are within the two pleural cavities. Between these two cavities is a double layer of pleura, known as the mediastinum; this separates the two pleural cavities from each other. As in dogs, cats and humans, in ferrets the mediastinum is tough and strong. In some species, this is not the case; in horses, the mediastinum is very weak, and any damage to the chest of a horse can easily lead to the collapse of both of the horse's lungs.

The abdominal cavity is sometimes referred to as being divided into the abdominal cavity and the pelvic cavity; this is rather confusing and misleading, since there is no physical division within the abdomen. This cavity is also lined with a serous membrane, called the peritoneum. All of the mammal's large interior organs, known collectively as the viscera, lie either behind the peritoneum (e.g. the kidneys), or in a fold of the peritoneum known as the mesentery; the peritoneal cavity contains a little serous fluid.

The pelvic diaphragm closes the posterior (towards the tail) part of the pelvis; it consists mainly of the muscles surrounding the muscular anal sphincter. This pelvic diaphragm is extremely important, as it has to maintain its shape despite the regular muscular straining involved with defecation. A perineal rupture may occur if there is any weakness or breakdown of the muscles in the pelvic diaphragm.

The pericardium contains the heart, and consists of a double layer of membrane; serous fluid lies between the two membranes, giving lubrication that allows the heart to move freely within the pericardium.

The Body's Systems

The mammalian body has eight systems:

- The skeletal system
- The muscular system
- The nervous system
- The endocrine system
- The respiratory system
- The circulatory or cardiovascular system
- The urogenital system
- The digestive system

In addition, the whole body is covered in integument (skin). In the ferret, the skin is very thick relative to similar species, varying in thickness from 0.5 mm to 1.8 mm (2/100th to 7/100th inch), and is at its thickest over the animal's shoulders. Kits have apocrine glands in the neck region; these help the jill to identify the kits as ferrets, and not prey.

The ferret has no sweat glands; in this species, the only scent glands are to be found in the animal's nose and footpads. The ferret's skin contains numerous sebaceous glands (i.e. producing fat or sebum). These glands constantly emit a sebaceous secretion that gives the ferret its characteristic musky smell. During the breeding season, the sebaceous secretion increases – in both hobs (males) and jills (females) – leading to an increase in the odour of the animal. The fat produced also causes the fur of albino and other white ferrets to become yellow, and gives the coat an oily feel.

The skin, with the exception of that of the lips and the nose, is covered with hair. This hair consists of both a short, soft undercoat, and long guard hairs. When the ferret moults, i.e. at the beginning of spring and then again at the beginning of autumn (dependent on the photoperiod under which the animal is kept), there are distinct marked changes in the animal's coat. In the summer, the darker varieties of ferret have a more pronounced coloration (i.e. they tend to look darker); the fur is winter is longer than in the summer, for obvious insulation qualities.

Each of the body's systems consists and is made up of various types of tissue, e.g. bone, muscular tissue, nerve tissue. In turn, these tissues are made up of three components:

1 Cells
2 Intercellular tissue
3 Fluid

The cell is the smallest unit of tissue within a mammalian body. Intercellular tissue, as the name suggests, is found between the cells, and is made up of fibres and membranes. All cells have fluid flowing around or bathing them.

There are four types of tissue within a mammalian body:

1 Connective
2 Epithelial
3 Muscular
4 Nervous

Connective tissue binds together all the other body tissues, and supports them, as well as acting as a transport system. There are various forms of connective tissue:

- Blood
- Bone
- Cartilage
- Dense connective tissue
- Loose connective tissue

The blood of the ferret, in common with other mammals, has many functions:

- Blood carries oxygen to, and carbon dioxide from, the body's cells.
- Blood carries digested food to the body's cells.
- Blood carries water to the body's cells.
- Blood carries waste materials away from the body's cells to the body's kidneys, from where it is excreted.
- Blood helps regulate the body's temperature by carrying and distributing heat throughout the body.
- Blood helps to stop haemorrhaging when it occurs, through its blood-clotting mechanism.
- Blood acts as a transport system for hormones and enzymes, moving them throughout the body.
- Blood protects the body from infections, using its blood-borne cells of the immune system, i.e. the transport of antitoxins and antibodies.
- Blood assists in the maintenance of the correct pH (acidity) in the tissues.

Blood is made up of both fluid and solid particles:

- Plasma (fluid)
- Blood cells

Plasma

Owing to its different functions, blood plasma has many constituents:

- Antibodies
- Antitoxins

12

- Enzymes
- Foodstuffs – the end products (such as amino acids, fatty acids and glucose) of food breakdown
- Gases – carried in solution; a large amount of CO_2 (carbon dioxide) is carried in plasma, although most of the oxygen transported around the body by the bloodstream is carried in the haemoglobin of the red blood cells
- Hormones
- Mineral salts (to maintain pH or acidity)
- Plasma proteins (helping maintain the osmotic pressure, thus preventing the leakage of fluid into tissue spaces)
- Waste products – mainly urea, which is taken to the kidneys for excretion from the body
- Water

Blood Cells

There are three types of blood cell:

- Red blood cells – erythrocytes
- White blood cells – leucocytes
- Platelets – thrombocytes

Red Blood Cells – Erythrocytes
Red blood cells contain haemoglobin, an iron-containing protein. This is what gives these cells their red coloration, and enables them to carry oxygen; haemoglobin enriched with oxygen is referred to as oxyhaemoglobin. While a ferret kit is in the jill's womb, red blood cells are made in the kit's bone marrow, liver and spleen; after birth, a ferret's red blood cells are only made in the animal's bone marrow.

The level of red blood cell production is governed by the amount of oxygen that reaches the tissues; when there is a low level of oxygen at the tissues, the ferret's kidney secretes a substance that kick-starts the bone marrow to produce extra red blood cells.

White Blood Cells – Leucocytes
Leucocytes are larger than red blood cells, and their chief function is to help the ferret's body to fight micro-organisms that can cause disease.

Platelets – Thrombocytes

These are cell fragments, and not 'true' cells; they play a major role in the ferret's blood-clotting mechanisms. Thrombocytes are also formed in the ferret's bone marrow.

It should be noted that vitamin K is essential for blood clotting, and when this vitamin is destroyed or its production decreased, the tendency for the ferret to bleed is increased. This happens when a ferret is fed carcasses of animals that have ingested large amounts of rodenticides such as Warfarin. In order to prevent unwanted clotting, the ferret's blood also contains heparin, an anticoagulant.

Bone

Bone is made of tissue, and there are two types of bone tissue – compact bone and spongy bone. Compact bone is what we normally think of as bone, i.e. a hard whitish substance. Bones are composed of this complex tissue, which is in the form of a series of 'canals' that run along the length of the bone. These canals are surrounded by layers of bone tissue and the centre canal carries the ferret's blood vessels, nerves and the lymphatics that serve that bone. Compact bone is found in the outer layer (cortex) of every bone.

These canal systems, known as Haversian systems, are different in spongy bone. The canals are spread far apart; the spaces between the canals are filled with red bone marrow, which in turn is made up of blood cells and fat. Spongy bone is found in the end sections of all of the ferret's long bones (see below); in short and fat bones, spongy bone forms the core. All bones are covered by periosteum, a tough, fibrous membrane.

Bones described as 'long bones' have a shaft and two ends. They have an outer layer of compact bone (the cortex), and spongy bone at the extremities; this is what gives the bone its strength, while keeping the weight to a minimum. All long bones have a central cavity, filled with bone marrow, although the majority of the formation of blood cells takes place in the spongy bone tissue, which is at the ends of the long bones.

So-called 'flat bones' have two layers of compact bone, and a layer of spongy bone between these two layers. Flat bones include bones forming parts of the skull, the pelvis and the scapula.

The bones of the vertebral column are known as 'irregular bones', and consist of two layers of compact bone, with a layer of spongy bone between the two. The patella is a type of bone known as sesamoid bone; these bones develop within a tendon, and sometimes within a ligament. Cartilage is found mainly at joints and between bones; it consists of a dense, clear blue-white substance that is very tough. With the exception of elastic cartilage, cartilage is rigid.

Dense connective tissue, also know as fibrous tissue, consists of large numbers of collagen fibres. These fibres may be either arranged at random, with fibres running in all directions, or, as in tendons and ligaments, all arranged in parallel, which gives the tissue great strength. Muscles throughout the body are bound together by sheets of dense connective tissue. Loose connective tissue, often referred to as areolar tissue, is found between and around (i.e. surrounding) organs throughout the mammalian body. It forms the layer between the skin and the tissue beneath.

Cell Reproduction

There are two types of cell reproduction – mitosis and meiosis – and both are achieved by a process known as binary fission, i.e. they divide in half. In mitosis, the chromosomes within the nucleus of the cell replicate themselves, forming an identical set of chromosomes for each; the resulting cells are known as 'daughter cells'.

Mitosis is divided into four stages:

- Prophase
- Metaphase
- Anaphase
- Telophase

Furthermore, there is a 'resting stage' between cell reproduction, and this is known as the 'interphase'. During this interphase, the chromosomes are duplicated within the nucleus of the cell. Each chromosome consists of two identical chromatids joined together at the centromere. During interphase, the individual chromosomes of the cell are invisible.

During prophase, the long threads of deoxyribonucleic acid (DNA) become shorter and stouter, and thus become visible. The centrosome (a specialised area of condensed cytoplasm) replicates, and one of these moves to the opposite side of the nucleus.

During metaphase, the chromosomes line up along the equator (centre) of the cell, following the breakdown of the nuclear membrane. A nuclear spindle is formed by the two centrosomes; this consists of a series of threads that pass from the centrosome on one side of the cell to the centrosome on the other side of the cell.

In anaphase, the chromatids move to opposite ends of the cell after separating from each other.

In telophase, the cell resembles an egg timer, the cell membrane being nipped in at the waist. This leaves two identical sets of chromosomes on either side of the waist, and the cell then divides in to two daughter cells, with each cell being identical.

Meiosis is explained in the chapter on genetics.

The Skeletal System

The skeletal system consists of bones, cartilage and ligaments. Its job is to:

- Protect the body's vital organs
- Allow locomotion (movement)
- Give form and rigidity to the body
- Help maintain the essential chemical balance within the body
- Form red blood cells

Ferrets are vertebrates (i.e. they have a backbone), and have an endoskeleton, i.e. a skeleton within the integument (skin). For its size, the ferret's vertebrae are large, and the vertebral formula is C7, T15, L5(6), S3, Cy18. The vertebral formula is an expression in symbols of the number of vertebrae in each region of the spinal column. The letters stand for:

- C   – Cervical
- T   – Thoracic
- L   – Lumbar
- S   – Sacral
- Cy   – Coccygeal or caudal

See diagrams on pages 18 and 19 for more details.

There are three parts of the skeleton:

- Axial skeleton – skull, backbone, ribcage and breast bone
- Appendicular skeleton – limbs
- Splanchnic skeleton – bones that develop in soft tissue

The axial skeleton provides protection for various organs:

- Skull – protects the brain
- Ribcage – heart, lungs and liver
- Vertebral column – spinal cord

In the ferret, the cervical vertebrae (of which the ferret possesses seven) are larger than those of the thoracic region (fifteen). This is an adaptation that allows for the powerful musculature of the animal, which it needs to control its head, particularly during predatory actions (i.e. catching, holding and killing its prey). The ferret's thorax, with fifteen vertebrae, is long, and may have either fourteen or fifteen pairs of ribs; some ferrets have fourteen ribs on one side, and fifteen on the other. Whatever the number of ribs, the first ten pairs are attached to the animal's sternum, with the remainder forming the costal arch (a portion of the lower part of the chest). Many of the abdominal organs of the ferret are encased and protected by the thorax.

The ferret is renowned for its articulated vertebrae (bendy backbone), and the lumbar vertebrae are articulated to allow a large amount of dorsal movement, and yet limit lateral movement.

The ferret's tail consists of eighteen caudal vertebrae, with the first three forming the roof of the animal's pelvic canal; the second to the fifth caudal vertebrae are 'hollow' and enclose and protect both an artery and a vein. As the tail nears its end, the vertebrae become progressively smaller, giving the tail its tapered appearance.

The ferret is a quadruped (i.e. has four limbs); the limbs are short and all terminate in feet with five digits (toes), each of which has a pad and a non-retractable claw. The ferret is a plantigrade (i.e. walks on the flat of its foot as do humans, and not on its toes, unlike the dog, which is a digitigrade). Because of this, the claws may need occasional trimming, although many ferret keepers trim the claws too short and too often; this leads to the claws growing more, and thus requiring more attention.

The forelimbs are attached to the thorax by muscles; there is no

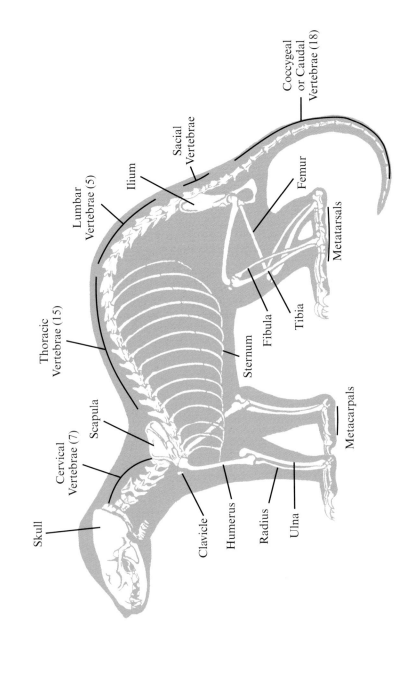

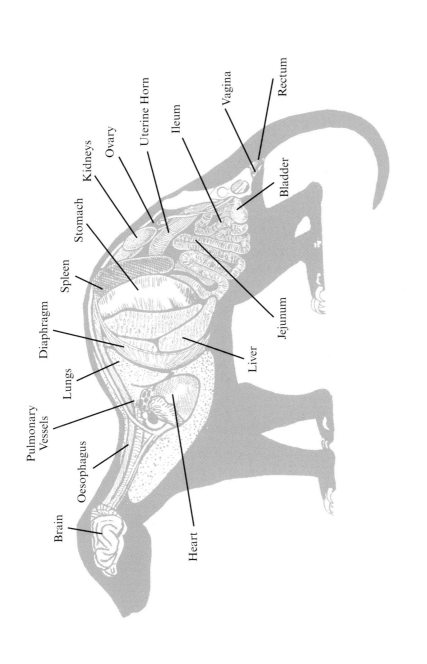

joint here. The rear limbs are attached to the pelvis via a ball and socket joint.

Locomotion is achieved when the muscles work against each other, or when a system of levers is created where muscles, attached to the skeleton, contract and relax; this allows the animal flexible movement.

Bone is a living tissue; it grows, renews cells and has a blood supply.

Protection

The body's skeleton is a system of rigid structures (bones and cartilage), which helps protect the body's vital organs, such as the brain, the heart, the lungs, the spinal cord and the urogenital system. Wherever two or more bones meet, a joint is formed; this may not always be a movable joint. There are three types of joint:

- Synovial joints
- Cartilaginous joints
- Fibrous joints

Where the surfaces of the bones in the joint are covered with hyaline cartilage, the joints are known as 'synovial joints'. In this case, the whole of the joint is covered and surrounded by a joint capsule; this joint capsule consists of two layers. The outer layer is a continuation of the periosteum, while the inner layer is made of synovial membrane; the latter lines the joint and the membrane secretes synovial fluid, to act as a lubricant. The synovial fluid also provides nutrients for the cartilage in the joint; in fit and healthy ferrets, the synovial fluid is more viscous than in the unfit ferret, where it is watery and much more sparse. Synovial joints may have ligaments on either the inside or outside of the joint capsule, to help stabilise the joint; usually these ligaments are on either side of the joint.

To help increase the movement range of the joints, while at the same time reducing wear and tear on the joints, the ferret's synovial joints may have one or more menisci (singular meniscus). These menisci are made from fibrous cartilage, and such joints occur in the ferret's jaw.

In some joints, the ferret's bones are connected by cartilage; these joints are known as cartilaginous joints. These may allow movement or may not. Those that do allow movement, such as in the inter-vertebral joints, are known as amphiarthroses, while those that allow little or no movement in the joint are known as synarthroses.

In the ferret's vertebral column, between and separating the adjacent vertebrae, are discs known as 'intervertebral discs'. These discs consist of two parts – a fibrous outer shell and a jelly-like inner substance – and act as a cushion between the vertebrae. As such, they help absorb any sudden shocks, and thus help prevent damage to the ferret's spinal cord.

The ferret's skull is made up of several pieces of 'flat bones', and these are joined together by dense fibrous connective tissue, which allows little or no movement; these joints are known as 'fibrous joints'.

Where joints can move, there are five categories of joints:

- Ball and socket joints
- Condylar joints
- Hinge joints
- Pivot joints
- Plane joints

The most freely movable joints (such as in the ferret's hips, where the rear legs join the pelvic girdle) are of a ball and socket design. The ferret's feet can be moved from a straight line, back to the straight line and then beyond (as in our wrist); such joints are categorised as condylar joints.

Where movement is only allowed in one direction, for example in the ferret's knee (stifle), the joint is referred to as a hinge joint; the joint flexes and then extends to an almost straight line. In joints such as the one between the ferret's radius and humerus (the radiohumeral joint), where rotation is allowed, the joint is referred to as a pivot joint. The small bones in the ferret's carpus and tarsus glide one bone over the other, allowing a limited amount of movement; these joints are known as plane joints.

The Muscular System

The muscular system is made up of the muscles of the body that are attached to the body's skeleton, and under voluntary control. There is more muscle elsewhere in the body, e.g. the visceral systems (digestive system, reproductive system, respiratory system and the urinary system), but this is not under voluntary control.

The Nervous System

The nervous system is one of the body's co-ordinating systems. It carries information to the CNS (central nervous system) and carries instructions away from it.

The Endocrine System

The endocrine system is the body's other co-ordinating and regulatory system, and again is a system for communication. It consists of a number of glands that produce chemical substances known as hormones (chemical messengers) that are carried in the body's blood; the organ to which the hormone is travelling is known as the target organ. It should be noted, however, that not all hormones are produced by the endocrine system.

The endocrine system consists of the following glands:

- The thyroid glands
- The pancreas
- The ovary
- The testes
- The adrenal glands
- The pituitary gland

The Thyroid Glands
The thyroid glands produce three hormones, including thyroxin. If *insufficient* thyroxin is produced, a condition known as myxoedema occurs. This condition leads to a lowered metabolic rate, and has the following symptoms:

- Animal is fat and sluggish
- Poor skin and coat

If *too much* thyroxin is produced, this will cause an increase in metabolic rate, leading to:

- Weight loss
- Increased heart rate
- Over activity
- Increased irritability

The Pancreas

The part of the pancreas included in the endocrine system is known as the Islets of Langerhans, and three hormones are secreted here:

- Insulin
- Glucagon
- Somatostatin

Insulin is secreted in response to a rise in blood glucose (e.g. after a meal); it lowers the blood level by increasing the uptake of glucose to the cells, and its storage as glycogen. A shortage of insulin (as in the condition diabetes mellitus), results in the body excreting glucose, via the urinary system. If this happens, the body will use fats and protein for energy.

Glucagon is secreted as a response to a fall in blood sugar; it stimulates the conversion of glycogen to glucose, thus raising the blood sugar level.

Somatostatin mildly inhibits the secretion of both insulin and glucagons, helping to reduce the huge swings of blood glucose levels that would otherwise be caused by the effect of one or other of these hormones. Somatostatin also reduces the secretion of digestive juices.

The Ovary

There are three hormones produced by the ovary:

- Oestradiol
- Progesterone
- Relaxin

Oestradiol is an oestrogen, and its function is to prepare the genital tract and external genitalia for coitus and the reception of fertilised eggs. Progesterone is essential for the maintenance of pregnancy; it acts on the lining of the uterus and on the mammary tissue. Relaxin is produced by the *corpus luteum* in the late stages of pregnancy; it causes the relaxation of ligaments around the birth canal, thus easing the passage of the foetus.

The Testes
Two hormones are produced in the testes:

- Testosterone
- Oestrogens

Testosterone is responsible for the development and maintenance of the male secondary sexual characteristics. Oestrogens, if produced in excess by the testes (as in tumours of the testes' cells) may 'feminise' the male.

The Adrenal Glands
Adrenaline is secreted by the adrenal glands, and prepares the body to deal with emergencies – 'Flight or Fight'. It increases the animal's heart rate and blood glucose level, and also increases the rate and depth of respiration, dilating the arteries that supply skeletal and voluntary muscle, thus allowing more blood to flow to and from these muscles. The extra flow of blood will help the muscles work better and faster, as the blood supplies energy and oxygen, and removes the potentially toxic products of the muscle's actions, e.g. carbon dioxide.

The Pituitary Gland
The pituitary gland produces the following hormones:

- Thyroid stimulating hormone (TSH)
- Growth hormone
- Adrenocorticotropic hormone (ACTH)
- Prolactin
- Follicle stimulating hormone (FSH)
- Luteinising hormone (LH)
- Anti-diuretic hormone (ADH or vasopressin)
- Oxytocin

Thyroid stimulating hormone regulates the uptake of iodine by the thyroid gland, the manufacture of thyroid hormones, and the release into the bloodstream of the thyroid hormones. The growth hormone controls the rate of growth in the young animal, and is involved in the production of proteins from amino acids. It regulates energy use within the body during periods of low food supply, by conserving glucose (for use by the nervous system) and stimulating the breakdown of fat for use by the rest of the body. Adrenocorticotropic hormone regulates the secretion of adrenocortical hormones. Prolactin stimulates milk production during late pregnancy and lactation.

Follicle stimulating hormone stimulates the maturation of ovarian follicles in the ovary. Luteinising hormone stimulates the development of the *corpus luteum* in the female, after ovulation. In the male, it controls the secretion of testosterone. Anti-diuretic hormone increases the absorption of water by the kidney tubules. This reduces the amount of urine excreted, thus increasing the amount of water retained. Oxytocin acts during pregnancy and parturition. It causes the contraction of the smooth muscle of the uterus, and also the ducts of the mammary glands.

The Respiratory System

Where a living creature exchanges gasses (gaseous exchange) between itself and its environment, this is described as respiration; respiration may occur internally or externally in the ferret. External respiration is where the ferret's gaseous exchange occurs between the air and the ferret's blood; where gaseous exchange occurs between the ferret's blood and its tissues, this is referred to as internal respiration.

The first job of the respiratory system is to draw in oxygen-rich air to the ferret's lungs; once inside the lungs, the oxygen in the inhaled air can be absorbed into the ferret's bloodstream. About 21 per cent of inhaled air is oxygen, with most of the rest (79 per cent) being nitrogen. The remainder of the inhaled air is made up of a minute amount of carbon dioxide (0.04 per cent), some water vapour, with minute traces of some other gases. After the air is exhaled, i.e. leaves the ferret's lungs, the oxygen level has dropped by about one-fifth to 16 per cent, while the carbon dioxide levels have increased by over 100 times to 5 per cent. The amount of water vapour may well have increased, but the percentages of other gasses remain the same as that in inhaled air.

The ferret's respiratory system consists of:

- The nose and nasal cavity
- The pharynx
- The larynx
- The trachea
- The bronchi
- The bronchioles
- The alveolar ducts and the alveoli

The ferret's nasal chamber, into which the oxygen-rich air is drawn, starts at the nostrils (external nares) and extends to the area where the inhaled air enters the pharynx (known as the internal nares). Down the centre of the nasal chamber, and dividing it into left and right nasal chambers is the nasal septum. Two bones extend into the nasal chamber; these are covered with a ciliated (hairy) mucous membrane. These two bones and their covering help to warm and moisten the air passing over them. The cilia, tiny hairs, also act as a filter. This system ensures that air passing into the lower parts of the respiratory tract is clean, warm and moist.

This clean, warm moist air then passes over the pharynx and into the ferret's larynx, at the top of the trachea. The pharynx, the area at the back of the ferret's mouth, is used by both the respiratory system and the digestive system, and there are also other openings into the pharynx. These openings are the mouth, two Eustachian tubes (from the ferret's middle ear), the oesophagus and the larynx.

The Circulatory or Cardiovascular System

The cardiovascular system consists of the ferret's heart and the blood vessels, and allows the circulation of blood around the ferret's body. Closely allied to the circulatory system is the lymphatic system; this carries lymph (excess tissue fluid) from the periphery back to the circulatory system.

The heart, which in the ferret is cone-shaped, is a folded piece of muscular tubing that is modified into a four-chambered pump that circulates the ferret's blood. This circulatory system can be divided into two parts – the pulmonary and the systemic. The pulmonary circulation system takes deoxygenated blood from the heart to the lungs. In the lungs, the blood gives up its load of carbon dioxide, and takes on oxygen; the blood then returns to the heart, and enters the systemic circulation. The systemic takes the newly oxygenated blood from the heart to the cells, tissues and organs in the rest of the ferret's body. The oxygen carried in the systemic blood is used by the cells, tissues and organs, and exchanged for carbon dioxide; this deoxygenated blood is then taken by the systemic, back to the heart.

Within the circulatory system are three types of blood vessels:

- Arteries
- Veins
- Capillaries

Arteries are large blood vessels that carry blood from the heart. They have thick walls, containing smooth muscle (i.e. muscle over which the ferret has no control); arteries can constrict or dilate to allow a greater or lesser flow of blood to particular tissues or organs. It is a common misunderstanding that arteries always carry oxygenated blood; this is not true. The blood in the pulmonary arteries is deoxygenated, and is carried away from the heart to the lungs, where it will be oxygenated, before being returned to the heart in the pulmonary veins; veins are large, thin walled blood vessels that carry blood to the heart.

As the arteries divide around the ferret's body, they decrease in size, and are referred to as arterioles, and these lie within the organs that they are supplying with blood. In the tissues, the blood vessels get even smaller, in order to allow gaseous exchange; they also have very thin walls, and are called capillaries. These capillaries form a network, known as the capillary bed, within the tissue, to allow gaseous exchange with all of the cells of the tissues. Within the tissues are small veins, called venules, which receive deoxygenated blood from the capillary bed.

Because veins have no muscles in the walls, they are supplied with valves, to prevent the back-flow of the blood. In the ferret's limbs, the veins have many such valves, although within the ferret's internal organs, veins have very few valves.

Not all of the ferret's tissues have a network of capillaries; the ferret's brain, heart and kidneys have end arteries. End arteries are capillaries that branch rather like the branches on a tree. They get smaller and smaller, but never join up with one another. The reason for end arteries in these three major organs is to protect against sudden drops in blood pressure, such as may occur after a major accident and its consequent blood loss. Other organs of the body can survive a period of low blood flow and vasoconstriction (the decrease in the calibre or bore of the blood vessels), allowing the ferret's body to divert the blood to these three vital organs, which cannot survive such a restricted supply of blood. As in all things, there is also a downside and disadvantage to this system of end arteries. If a blood clot or similar obstruction occurs, the blood will not be able to get to the tissue, and the tissue will there-fore die.

The Urogenital or Urinary System

The urogenital system removes waste – including water – from the ferret's body. It consists of:

- The kidneys
- The ureters
- The bladder
- The urethra

The Kidneys

The ferret has a pair of kidneys; they are situated against the dorsal (back) wall of the ferret's abdomen, and attached to the abdomen by a covering of fibrous tissue, known as a 'capsule'. The two kidneys lie on either side of the ferret's vertebral column, aorta and the vena cava (a large blood vessel). The ferret's right kidney is embedded in the liver and attached to the body wall. As in humans, the kidneys are kidney bean-shaped; this is not so in all species. The indented part of each kidney is known as the hilus; it is at the hilus that blood vessels, nerves and the ureters enter or leave the organ. There is a difference in size between the sexes; in the hob, the average weight of a kidney is 4.5 g, while in the jill, the average weight is 3.7 g. The ferret's kidneys are well supplied with blood, which enters from the aorta through the renal artery; blood leaves the kidneys via the renal vein, from where it joins the caudal vena cava.

The ferret's kidneys have five main functions:

- The formation of urine. This involves the excretion of waste and excess materials from the ferret's body; this includes water.
- The production of the enzyme rennin.
- The conversion of vitamin D to an active form (see Chapter 3 – Nutrition and Feeding).
- The production of the hormone erythropoietin.
- Helping to maintain the body's pH (other organs also help maintain the pH levels within the ferret's body).

Urine is formed within the kidneys, by the filtering of the ferret's blood passing through these two organs. The urine is then carried away from the kidneys via two ureters (one from each kidney) to the ferret's bladder, where the urine is stored before being disposed of through the ferret's urethra. The ferret's bladder is a distensible (stretchy) bag, which can hold a surprising amount of urine.

The Liver

The ferret's liver is large, relative to the animal's size, with six lobes; the gall bladder lies between two of these lobes. The liver produces bile, which is stored in the gall bladder or cholecyst, a pear-shaped organ that stores bile until it is required by the body (for digestion). It is connected to the ferret's liver and the duodenum by the biliary tract. The bile is stored in the gall bladder between meals, and upon eating is discharged into the duodenum, where it aids in digestion.

The liver is often referred to as 'the largest gland in the body', and receives blood from two sources:

- A branch of the aorta (20 per cent)
- Veins in the hepatic portal system (this blood carries many of the products of digestion)

The liver performs many functions for the body. For example:

- Protein metabolism
- Urea formation
- Carbohydrate metabolism
- Fat metabolism
- Formation of bile
- Detoxification and conjugation of steroid hormones
- Vitamin storage
- Production of heat
- Iron storage
- Regulation of amino acids and proteins
- Formation of cholesterol
- Elimination of sex hormones
- Filtration of blood
- Mineral storage (e.g. iron, copper)

Protein Metabolism
Many of the plasma proteins are synthesised in the liver, as are fibrinogen and other proteins involved in blood clotting.

Urea Formation
Ammonia (the toxic waste product of protein breakdown) is converted to urea, which is far less toxic than ammonia.

Carbohydrate Metabolism
Blood sugar levels need to be kept within very narrow limits, as surplus is stored in the liver as glycogen. This surplus can be released into the bloodstream as energy is required by the body.

Fat Metabolism
Some lipids required by the body are synthesised in the liver, and fatty acids are metabolised for energy production.

Vitamin Storage
Vitamins are either fat-soluble (A, D, E and K), or water soluble. The liver is the main storage for fat-soluble vitamins, and even some water-soluble vitamins (e.g. B_{12}).

Production of Heat
As part of homoeostasis, the liver helps regulate the body's temperature.

The Male Reproductive System

The reproductive system enables the animal to reproduce, and in the male consists of:

- The epididymes (singular – epididymis)
- The penis
- The prepuce
- The prostate gland
- The scrotum
- The testes (or testicles)
- The urethra
- The vasa deferentia (singular – vas deferens)

The male reproductive system produces, stores and nourishes sperm, and then transports these sperm into the jill's genital tract, where the sperm will fertilise the jill's ova.

The scrotum in the ferret lies at the base of the penis, and is a pouch or pocket of skin. This pouch is divided into two, with each cavity containing and holding a testis and an epididymis. The epididymis is a long, cord-like construction, with a coiled duct; the epididymis stores, transports and matures the hob's spermatozoa.

The testes develop while the ferret is a foetus, from gonads that have the potential to become either ovaries or testes. They start their life in the ferret's abdomen, just behind the kidneys. As the gonads develop into testes, they move downwards through the abdomen, through an opening in the abdomen wall, known as the inguinal ring, and then lie in the scrotum. In the ferret's scrotum, the testes are surrounded by a double layer of peritoneum; these layers are known as the vaginal sac, with the wrappings known as tunics. Attached to the testes are the 'tubes', which will carry blood, sperm and nerves.These tubes run through the inguinal ring; these tubes also include the vasa deferentia. Sometimes, one or both testes may not complete their journey; in such cases, one or both testes may remain in the abdominal cavity, or may become lodged just under the ferret's skin, near to the penis. A hob with only one testis descended is known as a monorchid, while a hob with neither testis descended is known as a cryptorchid. In the case of a cryptorchid, only the vaginal sac has managed to pass though the inguinal ring.

Within the ferret's penis is an os penis (a j-shaped bone); the os penis, or baculum, is a characteristic of many carnivorous species, and other groups of mammals, and in the ferret may measure as much as 45 mm (almost 2 in). The function of the os penis is to stiffen the penis, aiding coitus; unfortunately, when the ferret requires a urethral catheter for medical reasons, the os penis can cause severe difficulties. Down the centre of the penis is a tube – the urethra – along which will pass both urine and seminal fluid. The urethra and penis are both part of the hob's sexual reproductive system, but also part of the hob's urinary system.

Over the top of the penis is a fold of skin, known as the prepuce; the surface of the prepuce is hairy, while the internal skin is smooth. When the hob is engaged in coitus, the penis extends beyond and outside the prepuce. The penis is withdrawn back into the prepuce by a muscle known as the retractor penis muscle.

At the base of the penis, and surrounding the neck of the bladder, is a prostate gland. At the same level, the vasa deferentia connect to, and open into, the ferret's urethra. The prostate gland produces a large proportion of the seminal fluid of the hob's ejaculate. Where there is an enlargement of the prostate, this can cause an obstruction to the passage of urine, as well as obstructing the passage of faeces. In exceptional cases, where the prostate has enlarged to a great extent, the prostate may pass forward into the ferret's abdomen. If this is the case, a veterinary surgeon will be able to palpate the ferret's abdomen, and detect the problem.

The Female Reproductive System

The female reproductive system comprises:

- The vagina
- The vestibule
- The ovaries (two)
- The fallopian tubes (oviducts)
- The uterus (horns, body and cervix)
- The clitoris
- The vulva

The jill's reproductive system produces eggs (ova), which will be fertilised in her fallopian tubes, after which they will be transported to the horns of the uterus, where they will be implanted. In the uterine horns, the fertilised ova (the zygotes) will develop throughout the gestation period (pregnancy) to produce foetuses.

A jill's ovaries lie in her abdomen, one on each side, just behind her kidneys. Each ovary is attached to the dorsal (i.e. back) wall of the jill's abdomen by an ovarian ligament (suspensory ligament), via the kidney capsule. Within each of her ovaries, the jill has many primary ovarian follicles; each of these has the capability to develop into a ripe ovarian follicle, or Graafian follicle. While some species (normally) only release one follicle at a time, in the ferret, groups of follicles are released together; each follicle contains one ovum and a large amount of fluid.

When the jill ovulates (jills are induced ovulators – see Chapter 8), the follicles rupture, releasing the ova contained within them. After ovulation, there may be some bleeding into the ruptured follicle, but shortly afterwards, the cells of the follicular wall multiply and form a solid barrier, the *corpus luteum.*

The jill's ovaries are enclosed by the oviducts, which capture the released ova. The jill ferret has two long and tapering uterine horns, which join and fuse directly in front of the jill's cervix, forming a short body. The cervix is a muscular organ; it acts as a sphincter, closing the uterus, except during mating and parturition (birth or kitting).

The jill's vagina is extremely stretchable and is joined to the jill's rectum at one side and her urethra at the other (i.e. at top 12 o'clock and bottom 6 o'clock); the connection is by loose connective tissue. The vagina extends from the jill's cervix to the outside of her body, at the urethral opening. All of the vagina is contained in the jill's pelvis and extends backwards from the cervix, to where it bends sharply downwards at the level of the urethral opening to reach an area known as the vestibule. The vestibule is the place where both the jill's genital and urinary systems meet, both using the vestibule. The vestibule wall is extremely muscular, and once coitus has taken place, the muscles hold the hob's penis, forming a 'tie'.

The external opening of the jill's urogenital tract is endowed with a pair of vulval lips, which are normally soft, but become engorged and enlarged when the jill is in oestrus (in season). When a jill is in season, her vulva may measure over 1 cm (½ in) in diameter. At the base of the vulva lies the female equivalent of a penis – the clitoris; in the jill, this is very well developed. The outside boundary of the vulva is formed by the labia. The jill's urethra leaves her bladder and joins the external opening at the vaginal vestibule.

The Digestive System

The digestive system of the ferret is typical of carnivores, and is described as a visceral system, i.e. it consists of large organs that are within the abdomen. The function of the digestive system is to break down complex foods into simple compounds; this allows the ferret's body to absorb the foods. Once the foods have been broken down and absorbed, the digestive system then excretes the waste material.

The digestive system of the ferret starts at the mouth (which is large in comparison to the overall size of the animal), and finishes at the ferret's anus; to prevent dislocation of the jaw when the ferret

Lactation

Jill ferrets have two rows of three to five (normally four) nipples, as do the hobs but, of course, the hobs do not and cannot produce milk, as they do not have mammary glands. When a jill is pregnant, her mammary glands will start swelling as they produce milk; this does not, however, take place until very shortly before the jill is due to kit. A jill can feed more kits than she has nipples.

CHAPTER THREE

NUTRITION AND FEEDING

Feeding

It is a sad fact that, in the twenty-first century, many people feel that they don't need to understand or even know the reasons for feeding a balanced diet to themselves or their animals. Too many people are content to simply buy easy food, and give little thought to the consequences of such a diet, hence the dangerously high number of both people and pets that are clinically obese. If you are to successfully breed an animal, it must be fit; fitness and nutrition are inextricably linked. A fit, healthy animal will produce fit and healthy animals, and a balanced diet is essential for a long and healthy life.

Here in the UK, it was common, until quite recently, for many ferret owners to feed their animals on milk sops (bread and milk); unfortunately, some misguided or uncaring people still do so today. Those ferret keepers who still feed milk sops will tell you that they have sound reasons for so doing. The first 'reason' they will give is that, if one regularly fed meat to a ferret, it would give the animal a taste for flesh – and the animal would then be more inclined to bite the hand of the human keeper, making the ferret totally untameable. In the case of rabbiting ferrets (still one of the most common reasons for keeping a ferret in Great Britain) a ferret fed on a meat diet would, according to the adherents of a milk sop diet, make an extra effort to catch the rabbits it was chasing in the burrow. Another 'reason' given is that milk sops are a natural diet for ferrets. Obviously, none of these arguments, of course, are true. How on earth anyone can think that milk sops are natural for a ferret beggars belief; how often has anyone seen a ferret buying loaves of bread and bottles of milk in a shop – but how else could they obtain such items? Neither will the feeding of meat lead to the ferret biting the human hand, or killing and eating the rabbits it should be bolting from their subterranean refuge. It is foolish to give any animal a specific diet without first having investigated and obtained an understanding of that animal's nutritional requirements; with many ferret owners it would seem that the main reason for giving these poor diets is the low cost.

Over the years I and many other ferret owners and breeders have tried to find a good diet for our ferrets; good in that it is healthy for them, affordable for the keepers, and readily available. At the National Ferret School, we have probably tried most 'ferret diets', except milk sops, in which we have never believed, as we are only too aware of the nutritional deficiencies of such a diet. Fed a proper diet, the ferret's faeces will be dark, solid and have little smell, and the ferret will probably live for ten or more years (we have had several ferrets that have lived more than thirteen years). When fed milk sops, the faeces are almost liquid, very pale in colour, and extremely smelly; in other words, the ferret is living with perpetual diarrhoea – not a pleasant prospect. In addition, the ferret will lead a very unhealthy and short life (as short as three to five years).

A Balanced Diet

Before going any further, it is worth considering what constitutes a 'balanced diet'. All animals require certain items in their diet, with quite large differences between species. All animals require water, fat, carbohydrate, protein, fibre, some minerals and some vitamins. These requirements are not static; they will change with the ferret's age, lifestyle and physiological state, and so they will need to be adjusted and 'tweaked' throughout the ferret's life. A ferret fed on a balanced diet will lead a long, active and healthy life, more than repaying you for the cost of its diet. While feeding an imbalanced diet may not cause problems for many ferrets, the deleterious effects will be readily observed in a breeding programme, particularly with lactating jills, where the greater nutrient demand cannot be met by the jill's poor diet.

The main components of a balanced diet are:

- Proteins
- Vitamins
- Minerals

- Carbohydrates
- Fats
- Fibre
- Water

In general, a ferret requires:

- Water – essential for all life
- Protein (30–40 per cent) – for tissue and muscle growth and repair
- Fat (about 20 per cent) – for heating the body, and providing energy for life
- Iodine (3–5 mg/kg)
- Calcium (1–3 per cent) – for teeth and bones[*]
- Phosphorous (1 per cent) – for teeth and bones[*]
- Sodium chloride (salt) (1 per cent) – a vital mineral that acts as an electrolyte regulating the balance of water inside and outside cells
- Magnesium (level depends on calcium:phosphate ratio)
- Zinc (about 100–220 mg/kg)[**]
- Fibre (20–25 per cent) – as an aid to digestion
- Vitamin A (about 1000–4200 iu/kg) – this is a fat-soluble vitamin that plays essential roles in vision, growth and development, healthy skin, hair and mucous membranes, immune functions and reproduction
- Vitamin B_1 (Thiamine) (amount not yet determined)
- Vitamin B_2 (Riboflavin) (amount not yet determined)
- Vitamin B_6 (Pyridoxine) (amount not yet determined)
- Vitamin B_{12} (Cyanocobalamin) (about 1–13 μg/kg))
- Vitamin D (about 65–325 iu/kg), dependent on the calcium/phosphate ratio fed to the animal
- Vitamin E (about 250 mg/kg) – promotes normal growth and development, acts as an anti-blood clotting agent, and promotes normal red blood cell production
- Vitamin K (amount not yet determined)

---

[*] The ferret requires a calcium:phosphorous ratio of at least 1:2, and a sufficient daily dose of vitamin D to help the body assimilate the calcium.
[**] A deficiency in zinc may lead to skin lesions in kits.

Water

The importance of giving all ferrets constant access to a supply of fresh clean water cannot be over-emphasised; without it the ferret will not thrive. Where ferrets have only limited access to potable water, then the animals are in danger of kidney failure, since water is essential to help the kidneys function – getting rid of the toxic ammonia in the body and flushing it out of the body, as urea contained within the urine, which is composed mainly of water. Ferrets fed on a dry food diet will require more water, but even those fed on a meat/flesh diet will still require quite large quantities of water. Water is best delivered via bottles, hung on the outside of the cage, or an automatic watering system (see Chapter 5).

Proteins

Proteins are made from amino acids, and are essential for growth and tissue maintenance. In ferrets, proteins should form between 30–40 per cent of the diet of adults, while kits and young ferrets require a minimum of 35 per cent protein in their diets. Proteins suitable for ferrets are present in meats, eggs and milk. There are many different proteins, all consisting of different arrangements of about twenty amino acids, but it is not necessary to differentiate between them here, except to emphasise that the ferret is an obligate carnivore; it is designed to eat, and properly digest, meat/flesh.

It should be obvious that, while all ferrets require a high protein diet, this is even more important when considering nursing mothers, their kits and young ferrets in general; males used for stud also require a higher protein content in their diet. Ferrets that lead an active lifestyle (e.g. those used for rabbiting or for ferret racing), on a regular basis, will need higher levels of proteins. In nursing or pregnant jills, the level of proteins should be increased to between 35–40 per cent of her dietary intake.

Carbohydrates

Carbohydrates provide the body with heat and material for growth. As they are made up of carbon, hydrogen and oxygen (which combine to form cellulose, starch and sugar), excess amounts are stored as fat in the body, and can therefore lead to obesity if fed in excess on a regular basis. Obesity can and does cause medical problems, and will also inevitably lead to difficulties in the ferret's breeding. Carbohydrates are present in plant material; such material is available to carnivores via the stomach contents of their prey, as well as by direct ingestion of plant material. Recent research suggests that ferrets fed on a high fat/high protein diet do not require carbohydrates.

Vitamins

Vitamins are chemical compounds, essential for growth, health, normal metabolism, and general physical well-being. Many vitamins play an important part in completing essential chemical reactions in the body, forming parts of enzymes (chemical catalysts). Some vitamins form parts of hormones, which are the chemical substances that promote the health of the body, and reproduction.

Vitamins are divided into two types – water-soluble and fat-soluble. Water-soluble vitamins (B and C) cannot be stored in the body, and excess water-soluble vitamins are excreted. Every day's food intake must contain the day's requirements of these vitamins for the ferret. Fat-soluble vitamins (A, D, E and K) can be stored in the body; if more are taken in at one time than the ferret requires, fat-soluble vitamins can be stored for use when the body needs them. It should be noted, however, that an excess of such vitamins may cause toxic levels to accumulate in storage areas such as the liver, and thus may lead to long term physical problems. A lack of essential vitamins will be detrimental to the ferret's health.

A lack of, or an insufficiency of, any vitamin is known as avitaminosis, and excess of a vitamin is referred to as hypervitaminosis. Avitaminosis A (insufficient amounts of vitamin A) in the ferret results in poor growth, muscular in-coordination (particularly of the ferret's hindquarters) and poor night vision. Avitaminosis A is also linked with opaqueness of the ferret's eye lenses. Liver is an excellent source of vitamin A.

Vitamin B is, in fact, a complex of water-soluble vitamins, including biotin, choline, folacin, niacin, thiamine, riboflavin, pantothenic acid, pyridoxine and vitamin B_{12}. Avitaminosis B will manifest itself in anorexia, vomiting, poor movement, heart problems, alopecia, poor weight gain, greying of fur, conjunctivitis, poor circulation and many other symptoms.

Vitamin D is often referred to as 'the sunshine vitamin', as some species, including ferrets, can synthesise this vitamin if exposed to full daylight on a regular basis. The amount of vitamin

D required is also dependent on the calcium:phosphorous ratio fed to the ferrets. Abnormal bone development is a typical effect of avitaminosis D.

Vitamin E is found in the yolk of eggs, and in certain vegetable oils. A lack of this vitamin can cause infertility, heart and circulation problems and skin complaints; feeding too many eggs can also cause problems for ferrets (see below).

Vitamin K is necessary for normal blood clotting in ferrets.

Fat

Fat affects the palatability of food, and provides the ferret's body with energy. However, given too much, the body will store fat in the tissues. This can lead to many problems, including mating difficulties, heart problems and the re-absorption of foetuses. Fat gives approximately 2.4 times more energy (calories) per gramme than does carbohydrate. In normal circumstances, about 20 per cent of fat in a ferret's diet is sufficient, with about 15 per cent of this fat being in the form of unsaturates, which contain essential fatty acids such as linoleic acid. The downside of unsaturated fatty acids is that they can quickly become rancid, resulting in the feed becoming unpalatable and leading to the destruction of vitamin E in the feed. If feeding a pelleted diet, then it is vital that it contains adequate levels of vitamin E, and that the feed is stored correctly, i.e. in an airtight container, in a cool, dark place.

Fibre

Fibre (or roughage, to use its old-fashioned name) is essential for the well-being of the ferret's digestive system. It keeps the ferret 'regular', i.e. producing the correct amount of faecal material, and excreting it from its body; this will help prevent many of the diseases (including cancer of the bowel) with which some ferrets are afflicted. Fibre for the ferret is to be found in the fur and feathers of its prey.

Minerals

The mineral calcium, essential for sound and strong teeth and bones, is found in liver, milk and milk products, egg shells, fish, and snails; calcium is also found in the bones and teeth of all animals. Phosphorous is found in liver, milk and milk products, and fish, and is also essential for teeth and bones.

If the ferret's feed does not contain sufficient levels of iodine, the ferret may develop goitre (an enlargement of the ferret's thyroid gland, causing a swelling in the front section of the neck), a deformed skeleton, alopecia and timidity. Insufficient levels of iodine can also lead to the delayed shedding of the ferret's deciduous teeth.

Iron and copper are both essential to ferrets (copper is necessary for the body to absorb iron, an essential element of haemoglobin – the oxygen-carrying constituent of the red blood cells). A lack of these minerals can result in emaciation, anaemia, poor fur quality (tends to be rough) and poor coloration of the ferret's under-fur.

Magnesium deficiency in ferrets may result in anorexia, poor weight gain, irritability or weak muscles. Insufficient levels of potassium in a ferret's diet may result in poor/retarded growth, muscular paralysis, or restlessness. Sodium and chlorine are essential to a ferret's normal physiological performance. Deficiencies may result in a number of symptoms, including tiredness, retarded growth, weight loss, excessive water intake and dry skin. Zinc helps prevent alopecia, poor growth, anorexia and emaciation.

*   *   *

As can be seen from the foregoing information, a balanced and truly complete diet for ferrets is complicated, and most ferret keepers will struggle to provide this essential dietary regime unless they are feeding a commercial diet specifically designed for ferrets. However, as some ferret keepers and breeders wish to avoid such diets, we will look at some possible alternatives.

Diets

Ferrets are carnivores, a word derived from the Latin *carnis*, meaning flesh, and *vorare*, to devour. As such, their natural diet is one of flesh, i.e. whole carcasses of animals – mammals, birds, reptiles, fish, amphibia and even some invertebrates. Where it is possible to feed ferrets with an extremely wide range of prey species, and on a regular basis, such a diet will be highly likely to provide a balanced and complete diet. However, as very few people will be able to guarantee obtaining such a wide and varied number of prey animals on a regular basis, most ferrets fed such a diet will inevitably be malnourished to a greater or lesser degree.

If you decide to feed your ferrets with such a diet, do not throw a complete carcass (e.g. a rabbit or chicken) into their cage, leaving it until it is all eaten, unless there is a large number of ferrets in that cage, the ferrets being able to eat the complete animal within 24 hours. Such a practice, which is unfortunately all too common, is bad husbandry. Eventually, such practices will inevitably lead to ill health and possibly the death of one or more of your ferrets; breeding programmes will not be successful in the long term. Unless you keep a fairly large number of ferrets in one court, carcasses of all but the smallest animals should be cut into portions, all with the fur left on (fur is an important part of the dietary fibre needed to keep the ferret's digestive system in good condition). Leaving the animal's organs intact is also beneficial. Where this is done, you should check for such diseases as liver fluke, which is visible as white dots on the infected animal's liver. Any infection or disease within the animal should lead to the rejection of that carcass for feeding. For a litter of kits that are eating flesh, a full rabbit (minus its guts) will be perfectly acceptable, and will help their development, as well as keeping them active.

If you are to feed your ferrets on a diet of carcasses, it is essential that you cultivate the friendship and favours of friends and farmers who shoot; such people can often be relied upon to provide the cadavers of pest species, or even game species that are too badly shot for human consumption, or have been badly chewed by a hard-mouthed dog. If you use your ferrets for hunting, then your own catch of rabbits can be utilised. Unless you are incredibly lucky, there will inevitably be times when it is impossible to provide all of the food for your ferrets; as a regular supply of good quality food is required for the animals' well-being, and your peace of mind, this should be considered well before embarking on such a dietary regime.

Day-old Chicks/Cockerels

One of the items that some sources quote as being a good staple for ferrets is day-old chicks (cockerels). These are widely available throughout the Western world, as they are the culled male birds from hatchings of eggs to supply new stock to egg producers. Sold mainly as food for raptors – owls, hawks etc. – their cost is extremely low. However, there are great risks to ferrets fed on a diet in which day-old chicks feature on a regular basis.

Medical and veterinary research indicates that day-old chicks are very low in calcium, protein and fat, and contain very little vitamin E. The feeding of day-old chicks has also been shown to cause problems such as hypocalcaemia, actinomycosis (a thickening and swelling of the neck), osteodystrophy, thiamine deficiency, posterior paralysis (the 'staggers'), and other maladies (see Chapter 10). Many years ago, I fed my ferrets with day-olds on a regular basis; I no longer feed any such food to my ferrets.

Dog and Cat Foods

Throughout the Western world, a ready supply of quality meat is available from supermarkets, in the shape of tinned dog and cat food, and many ferret keepers use this as a basis for their ferrets' diet. However, these foods are not designed for ferrets, and many will need to have vitamin and mineral supplements added to form a balanced and complete diet for ferrets.

In addition, many pet shops now sell 'pet meat' or brawn, of different flavours, and some of these brands can be fed. But again, many will require supplementing to ensure no long-term ill effects if these items are to be given to your ferrets regularly, or over a long period.

At the very least, I recommend that where tinned dog and cat foods (and other similar foods) are fed to ferrets, these foods be supplemented with the addition of a top quality vitamin and mineral supplement.

Dry Foods

The modern trend in animal nutrition is to feed 'complete diets'; in zoos, where the idea started, and for dogs and cats, these are now the most popular types of feeding. In some countries, this is also true for ferrets, since in recent years they have become so popular as to make it financially viable for pet feed manufacturers to produce balanced and complete pelleted diets for ferrets.

Usually made in pellet or 'muesli-type' form, the idea was originally driven by necessity, as zoos needed to be able to supply a wide range of animals with all of their nutritional requirements, and found it almost impossible to do so by feeding 'natural' foods, many of which were just not available locally, or on a regular basis. This was highly successful and it was not long before the pet trade took an interest in the idea.

Such diets are extremely convenient, have an acceptable smell, are appetising to all but the most pampered dog or cat, and really are a 'complete diet'. Add to that cheapness, ease of availability and storage, and the fact that tinned pet foods contain a lot of water, and it is obvious why complete dry feeds for pets have become so successful. However, unless you can obtain complete ferret diets, i.e. those designed specifically for the ferret, you will have to add supplements and be ever watchful for long-term deleterious effects on your ferrets. Deleterious effects caused by incorrect feeding can be so insidious that they are difficult to notice until it is too late, by which time, complete kennels of ferrets could have been made useless.

A warning of embarking on untested diets was given by BP Nutrition (UK) Ltd, at a symposium organised by ABWAK (the Association of British Wild Animal Keepers) on the management of canids and mustelids, in 1980. In the paper presented to the meeting, the story was told of mink farmers using a commercial diet for their animals that had not been proven with mink. At first, everyone was happy with the results but, after more than eighteen months of being fed on this diet, the mink began to exhibit serious problems, including stunted growth, poor fur, and reduced litter sizes. Research proved that these problems were a direct result of feeding an unsuitable diet to the mink. We should learn the lesson, and not feed diets or foods which are not intended for ferrets.

One of the advantages with feeding diets based on dried materials, is that they tend to produce more solid, drier and less smelly faeces, and this encourages a lot of ferret owners to supply them to their charges. Thanks to the undisputed fact that ferrets have become increasingly popular as pets in many countries, such as the UK and the United States, it is now possible to buy complete (dry) quality diets specifically designed and manufactured for ferrets. I have been feeding such a diet to my ferrets for over ten years, with no apparent deleterious effects on the animals' health, working ability or breeding success.

Complete Ferret Feeds

The best option for feeding domestic ferrets, these feeds are specifically designed for ferrets, and meet all of the species' nutritional requirements; complete ferret feeds have revolutionised ferret-keeping. It is now possible to supply ferrets with an easily

A top quality complete diet ferret food is the best way of ensuring well-nourished ferrets.

obtainable and affordable diet without the need to work hard at the task. Pet stores and even supermarkets now stock these feeds, and with ever more manufacturers launching ferret feeds, the area is highly competitive. As with all things, however, not all ferret feeds are of equal quality; ensure that the feed you purchase is of the correct nutritional balance and made with the finest ingredients.

Other Foods
Raw green tripe, the unprocessed stomachs of cows, is an excellent food for dogs, cats, ferrets and almost every other carnivore. In some countries, it is easily obtainable, with some pet shops selling it in 'tubes', minced, frozen and even in tins. However, since the bovine spongiform encephalopathy (BSE or 'mad cow disease') outbreaks in the UK, it has become very difficult to obtain green tripe directly from British abattoirs. Tripe also has a strong and disagreeable smell, and some people will not feed it solely for this reason. Ferrets are not deterred by the smell, and will eat it with gusto. As with all meats, always ensure the tripe is fresh and, if frozen, defrost thoroughly before feeding it, and always feed any meat as soon after defrosting as possible.

Heart, lights (lungs), cheek and udder can be bought reasonably cheaply, and make good ferret food but will require supplementing

49

with calcium and vitamins. Again its availability is being limited by the BSE scares. Liver is enjoyed by all ferrets, and has much nutritional value; however, it should not be fed in excess and *never* form a staple. Avoid liver and all other meats sold as 'pet food', which has been branded as 'unfit for human consumption', for whatever reason. My personal maxim is that, if meat is not fit for me to eat, it is not fit for my ferrets either.

Butchers, supermarkets, pet stores and other retailers often sell 'minced pet food'. This consists of many different sorts of meat minced up together and frozen, and will include offal, fat and waste. These meats tend to be high in fats, and should not be fed as a staple, although the high fat content will be useful in cold weather, or when the ferrets are working hard, as their calorific needs will be much higher than normal.

Fish is relished by ferrets, but should only be fed in limited quantities; avoid smoked, salty or fatty fish. Before feeding, all fish must be well filleted, as fish bones can easily become lodged in a ferret's windpipe, often with fatal results.

Eggs

In the wild, polecats (the wild ancestors of the domestic ferret) will eat eggs, and so some people argue that eggs must, therefore, be good for ferrets, as they are 'natural'. They therefore feed their ferrets with a regular diet of eggs, sometimes giving each ferret a full egg every day. In the wild, birds only lay their eggs at one time of the year and so polecats only have a limited capacity to find and eat eggs. Too many raw eggs (i.e. more than one per week for an adult ferret) may well have deleterious effects, causing diarrhoea and hair loss. Try feeding hard boiled eggs, complete with their shells, which are a good source of calcium, or even scrambled eggs; ferrets love them.

Adjusting the Diet

The ferret's diet will need to be adjusted to compensate for its lifestyle; a ferret kept indoors and not given much exercise will need far less energy food (i.e. carbohydrate and fat) than an animal kept outside and worked regularly. All animals will need more carbohydrate and/or fat in colder weather leading to colder ambient temperatures. Pregnant jills and young kits will require higher amounts of protein, fat and calcium.

Quantities

How much food should a ferret be given each day? This is a very difficult question to answer, as all ferrets have different requirements. The amount will also vary from season to season, and from day to day, depending on ambient temperatures, energy expended by the ferrets, and other factors. A general rule of thumb is to feed the ferrets with an amount that you think is correct, and then check on the food later in the day. If all of the food has been eaten, always remembering that ferrets are hoarders (some will have been secreted away in the nest box or elsewhere), feed a little extra next time. Ideally, there should still be a small amount of food left, to ensure that all of the ferrets have sufficient food for their needs. All leftovers must be removed at the end of each day, to avoid the risks of the ferrets eating food that has become contaminated.

The ferret's digestive system, like that of all carnivores, is short, and too large a quantity of food may result in much of it passing undigested through the ferret. Feed your ferrets regular meals, and this will result in less waste, less opportunity for the food to go off before they have a chance to eat it, less illness, and happy and contented animals. Ferrets should be fed daily, and fasted on one day each week; a fasting day is good for the health of all animals.

If feeding meat, in the summer, when it is warm, you should feed your stock in the evening; this will help prevent the food from going off before the ferrets have a chance to eat it. Where ferrets are fed a complete, balanced dry commercial diet intended and designed for ferrets, it is recommended that the ferrets are given food throughout the day, and allowed to eat *ad libitum*.

Special Dietary Requirements

As mentioned earlier, dietary requirements for ferrets will vary according to several factors. Stud males need to be fit and healthy, and to have plenty of energy; they require a diet high in fats (for energy) and protein (for energy and cell – sperm – production).

Jills used for breeding require sufficient nutrients to feed themselves and their developing kits. It is estimated that, where a jill does not get sufficient nutrients, it is possible that as many as 20–30 per cent of the kits die. Breeding jills require a high level of fats and a high level of proteins, along with high levels of calcium, throughout the pregnancy. During the final few weeks of her pregnancy, the jill's food intake may increase by as much as 25 per cent. It is essential, therefore, that such jills are fed a top-quality diet *ad libitum*; this should continue until all of the kits are weaned. Insufficient calcium during pregnancy and/or while the jill is feeding the kits, is likely to result in 'milk fever' – hypocalcaemia.

Kits and young ferrets grow at a tremendous rate, and so require a high calorie feed, rich in protein and calcium. At about three weeks, the kits will start to eat the food that the jill will carry into the nest. If the breeder is feeding one of the complete diet kibbles (biscuits), then a small quantity of this feed should be wetted with warm water, and mixed with a small quantity of pork (or similar) fat. We use fat dissolved in warm water or, even better, cooked high fat content minced meat (and the water in which it is cooked) is mixed with the dry feed before it is fed to the litter. This softened food should be fed on a twice-daily basis; this food will be easier for the kits to ingest, and will boost the fat content of the diet, and at the same time make the feed more palatable for the youngsters. Obviously, any of the food left over must be removed before it deteriorates and leads to food poisoning. Some of this food will also be ingested by the jill; this is helpful to her to maintain her body condition, and also her production of milk (lactation).

Water

Clean, fresh water is essential for all life, and arguably the most important constituent of a balanced diet. It is obvious, therefore, that a constant supply of clean fresh water must be available to your ferrets. Water is even more important to ferrets fed on a dry or semi-moist diet, for obvious reasons. Ferrets in general, and nursing jills, kits and older ferrets in particular, are highly susceptible to dehydration.

Although some breeders use dishes, water is best delivered in a drinking bottle with a stainless steel spout, of the type sold in pet stores as 1 litre 'rabbit drinking bottles'; these are ideal. The bottles must be emptied, cleaned and checked daily, ensuring that the water flows freely; the spout can easily become blocked with wood shavings, hay and even fur. Ensure that the bottle is securely

An external water bottle, fitted to a ferret cub.

fastened to the cage, on the outside, and check this fastening when checking the bottle. Dark-coloured glass, such as wine bottles, is a good method of slowing down the growth of algae on the inside of the bottle. Also, particularly in hard water areas, care should be taken to check for the build-up of lime scale, which can block drinking nozzles, pipes etc. Any build-up found should be removed as soon as practical, in order to prevent a major problem arising.

Daily checks must be made on all water bottles, especially in extremes of weather. During periods of very low temperatures, the water in the bottles may well freeze, and often this will cause a glass or plastic bottle to crack. We cover the bottles with insulating material to prevent them freezing; the one drawback with this, is that it is impossible to check the contents of the bottle without physically removing the covering every time. We feel that this is, however, a small price to pay for the peace of mind of knowing that the water is unlikely to freeze. In courts, where there are several ferrets living together, it is essential to have two or three bottles, and maybe even a water container such as is given to chickens.

About eight years ago, we installed an automatic watering system, and have found the investment in time, effort and money to be well worthwhile. The system has a header tank, which is filled directly from the mains water system; this feeds into the ferret cages via black tubing, onto the ends of which are fitted specialised drinking nipples. The black tubing helps prevent algal growth, and the nipples are constructed to allow proportional water flow (i.e. the harder the ferret pushes on the central spindle of the nipple, the more water comes out); in addition, the nipples do not allow any back-flow, thus eliminating the risk of cross infection via the drinking water reservoir. Also within the watering system, we have fitted several in-line filters, and each nipple is equipped with its own filter, making the system extremely hygienic in operation. I would recommend all breeders to investigate a system such as this. Whatever type of watering system is used, the nipples and tubes must be checked for blockages and also, particularly in areas of hard water, lime scale build-up.

*   *   *

The feeding of a high-quality, balanced diet is essential to the long-term well-being of ferrets. I recommend that a quality commercial ferret feed is used, to ensure that the ferrets in your care receive the correct nutrients, in a balanced diet.

If changing the ferrets' feeding regime, this must be done in stages, otherwise the change will cause upset to the animal's digestive system, leading to diarrhoea and dehydration. In young and old stock, such conditions can quickly lead to a rapid deterioration in the animals' condition, and even to the death of some or all of the animals. Even in fit and healthy mature ferrets, drastic and sudden changes in diet can lead to a loss of condition.

When changing the diet, do so over several days. On days one, two and three, mix 25 per cent of the new diet with the old feed; on days four, five and six, mix 50:50. Increase the amount of new feed to 75 per cent on days seven, eight and nine, and by day ten, the ferrets will be on the new diet with very few, if any, deleterious effects on the animals' health.

CHAPTER FOUR

CARE AND MAINTENANCE

The ferrets in your care need to be given attention throughout the year, on a daily basis. This will include feeding, maintenance, veterinary and prophylactic (preventative) treatment.

Daily/Weekly Care

Ferrets are creatures of habit, and will use the same area of their cage for defecation and urination; this area will require cleaning each day, and the soiled substrate (floor covering) removing and replacing with fresh material. We use a simple but effective system to help ease the burden of this task. We use plastic 'washing up' bowls, bought for very little cost from a hardware shop or supermarket. These bowls are approximately 450 mm x 300 mm (18 in x 12 in) and stand about 150 mm (6 in) high. We cut down two adjacent sides to about 50 mm (2 in) high. Ferrets like to back into a corner to defecate, raising their rear ends as they do so; the higher sides of the litter tray are placed into the corner of the cage, and prevent the excrement from going over the side of the tray.

In the litter tray, we place wood shavings to about 30 mm (1½ in) deep. The bowl is placed in the corner of the cub (hutch) furthest from the nest area; it is advisable to wedge the litter tray, perhaps using stones or similar, to prevent the ferrets from moving these trays. In wooden cubs it is possible to screw wooden slats to the floor of the cub, into which the litter tray can fit snugly. In larger cubs and courts, we place one of these litter trays in two or more areas; if necessary, we place rocks or branches around the litter tray to keep the ferrets from pushing the tray around the cage. For every litter tray we place in the cage, we have a second outside, always kept clean and ready for use. When we service the cage, we remove the soiled litter tray, and immediately replace it with a clean, fresh litter tray. The soiled litter tray is then thoroughly cleaned and the shavings replenished, and the tray is then ready for use the following day.

It is while carrying out the task of cleaning the latrine that we check on the inhabitants of the cage, and the condition of the cage itself. We clean the ferrets' water bottle(s) or other watering devices, and refill, checking to ensure that the water flows correctly. Also, we check the security of the cage – fastenings, hinges, wire netting, wood etc. Any faults are rectified on discovery, and not put off for another day.

While handling the ferrets, it is quite easy, and far from onerous, to carry out health and maintenance checks on the animals. On a daily basis, we check all of our ferrets for ailments and injuries; where they have been used for rabbiting and similar work, it is quite possible for the ferrets to have sustained one or more minor injuries, such as bites and scratches etc. Such injuries need to be treated on the day of the injury, but will need checking, in order to ensure that the injuries do not worsen (see Chapter 10 for details of first aid treatment of minor injuries in ferrets). If any deterioration is noted,

Ferrets need a constant supply of clean, fresh water.

wounds do not seem to be healing properly, or an infection appears to be setting in, veterinary advice should be sought.

Feet and Claws

The ferret's feet can easily become injured or damaged through its everyday activities. Holding the ferret, we examine the soles of the feet, the toes and the claws. Where detritus has adhered to the feet (very often between and around the ferret's toes) this should be carefully and gently removed. If the material has hardened, bathing the feet in warm water will usually soften the material sufficiently to allow its removal.

We always check the ferret's claws; contrary to the opinions of some ferret keepers, the claws do not need to be short. As the ferret is a plantigrade, i.e. the animal walks on the flat of its foot, rather than on its toes (digitigrade) like a dog, the claws will need to be slightly longer than most keepers imagine them to be. Where the ferret has opaque or clear nails, it will be easy to see where the blood vessels end; the claw should be about 3–5 mm beyond this point. Where the ferret's claws are dark or black, this is not easy to gauge, and novices at this task should seek guidance and help from more experienced ferret keepers or their veterinary surgeon.

If the claws do need cutting, then this operation should be carried out with care. If you do not have the relevant experience, then do not attempt this procedure; take the ferret to a veterinary surgeon or an experienced ferret keeper, who will do the job, and explain and demonstrate the procedure to you. Ferrets' claws should only be trimmed using a guillotine-style claw trimmer; scissor-type cutters can result in the claws being pulled out, rather than cut; I do not need to point out that such an accident would be extremely painful.

The ferret's claws are formed from thick horn, which is attached to skin tissue; this tissue is supplied with blood vessels and, if the claws are clipped too short, they will bleed. If this happens, the ferret will feel pain, and is quite likely to bite the hand restraining the animal. If such an accident does happen, the bleeding will need to be stemmed, and this can be achieved by applying direct pressure on the open end of the cut, i.e. the end of the claw. The application of a caustic pencil, or a tiny drop of 'super glue', will stem the flow if the application of pressure fails. If using super glue, extreme care must be exercised, to ensure that toes, fur and human fingers do not become fixed together. It is obvious that the animal should be restrained, and prevented from licking or smelling the glued claw, until such time as the glue has completely set. If in doubt, do not attempt any such procedure yourself; contact an experienced ferret keeper or your veterinary surgeon.

Fur

The ferret's fur, or pelage, should also be examined regularly. Many diseases, nutritional deficits and other ailments will manifest themselves as 'poor fur'. If the fur is greasy, or conversely dry and brittle, then there is probably a problem, and the afflicted ferret should be taken for examination by a veterinary surgeon. During the summer months, the ferret will produce increased amounts of sebaceous secretion from its sebaceous glands; these glands constantly emit a sebaceous secretion that gives the ferret its characteristic musky smell. However, during times when the ferrets are kept in a stimulatory photoperiod, the amount of secretion increases dramatically, leading to an increase in odour; this occurs in both hob and jill. The fat produced (i.e. in the sebaceous secretions) also causes the fur of albino and other white ferrets to become yellow, and gives the coat an oily feel.

The base of the fur should also be examined for signs of ectoparasites, such as fleas, ticks or lice. Many animal owners consider it an insult that someone should suggest that the animals in their care could be afflicted with 'dirty' parasites, but it is a fact that *any* animal can contract endoparasites ('worms' etc.), ectoparasites or both. Regular examination of the animal's pelage will help reveal the problem before it becomes serious. There are many proprietary brands of flea, lice and similar powders on the market, but it is often best to seek veterinary advice before using these, as some are obviously better than others, while some may not be suitable for use on ferrets. *Always* seek veterinary advice before treating kits and/or suckling jills.

Eyes

A healthy ferret will have shiny, dry eyes. Any excessive running (tears), or discharge should be investigated. If in any doubt about the health of a ferret's eyes, seek immediate veterinary advice.

Ears

The external parts of a ferret's ears are called pinnae (singular pinna), and should not present any problems. However, the inside of its ears will accumulate dirt and there will also be wax present. *Wax in the ears is normal.* In the UK, many exhibitors, conscious of the fact that their ferrets will lose marks for 'dirty' ears, often resort to scrubbing the ferret's ears, in an attempt to clean them. In so doing, the wax – designed by nature as a protectant – will be removed, and the ears made sore. Cleaning the ears of ferrets is often not necessary, and rarely advisable. If in doubt about the state of a ferret's ears, seek veterinary advice.

Teeth

The ferret is famous (or should that be infamous?) for its teeth, which are vital for helping the animal ingest food and, if the ferret works (i.e. hunts rabbits) for a living, for killing its prey and also for defending itself. In some areas, owners have their ferret's teeth removed, or at least the canine teeth. *This is cruel*, and definitely not necessary; if your ferret is inclined to bite you, this is because he has not been handled properly from an early age, or may indicate that he has inherited this poor behaviour from his parents. Whatever the cause, removal of a ferret's teeth is not good husbandry.

The teeth can easily become discoloured, particularly if the ferret is fed on a complete diet where the feed is coated with gravy or similar (as a part of the manufacturing process). Plaque can also build up on a ferret's teeth. Teeth that are stained may be more susceptible to decay, and so need to be cleaned. It is possible to purchase 'teeth cleaning' chews from pet shops, and these can often be useful in keeping the teeth in good order. If the ferret appears to have a problem with decayed or damaged teeth, veterinary advice should be sought.

Nose

The ferret's nose should be clean and clear, i.e. no congestion. Ferrets kept in straw may sometimes get a piece of the material up their nose, which will cause discomfort and soreness, and should be removed as soon as possible; this may often require the services of a veterinary surgeon. Where hay is used, there is a possibility of the seeds in the hay becoming lodged in the nasal passages. In this case, veterinary treatment is essential.

Worming
All ferrets are born with a worm (helminth) burden, and should be treated on a regular basis for worms. This is true of both flesh-fed ferrets and those fed on a complete, pelleted diet. Jills should be wormed prior to being used for breeding, and kits at six weeks of age.

Vaccinations
In some countries, it is common to vaccinate ferrets against a wide range of diseases. However, the main threat to a ferret's health and well-being is canine distemper (hard pad). This is particularly so where the ferret is walked on areas used by dogs, some of which may not have themselves been vaccinated against this killer disease. It is advisable to seek veterinary advice to be certain for the vaccinations necessary for your locale. In some areas, it is a legal requirement to have animals vaccinated against certain diseases. At the time of writing, there is currently *no* distemper vaccine licensed for use in ferrets in the UK; consult your veterinary surgeon for advice on this matter.

Minor Injuries
It is highly unlikely that a ferret will go through its entire life without suffering some minor injury. Such injuries – bites, scratches etc. – if treated promptly and efficiently, can be cured without long lasting consequences. Details of the most common injuries and illnesses are given in Chapter 10.

Bathing
Regular bathing of ferrets is unnecessary, and can result in a poor coat, particularly if harsh detergents are used. There are specific shampoos for use on ferrets but, to my mind, these are not a good idea for regular usage. Where the ferret has a specific diagnosed skin condition, a prescribed shampoo may be necessary, and so such ferrets should be referred to a veterinary surgeon.

Transporting a Ferret

It is often necessary to transport a ferret – to a show, for a day's hunting, to a veterinary surgeon etc. – and so it is advisable to have a 'carry box' for this job. Wooden or plastic carry boxes are widely

A good, strong and well-ventilated carry box is essential.

available and used for ferret transportation. Where a wooden box is used, it should be painted – both inside and outside – with non-toxic, waterproof paint; this will enable the box to be properly cleaned and disinfected on a regular basis, thus preventing the build-up of harmful pathogenic organisms, deleterious to the ferret's health.

Ensure that the box is large enough for the ferret's comfort, and has adequate ventilation. When transporting the ferret, in its box, in a vehicle, ensure that the box is never transported in direct sunlight. Carry boxes left in sunlight, even for a few minutes, will rapidly over-heat, killing the ferret inside.

CHAPTER FIVE

HOUSING

The housing of ferrets is very much a matter of personal choice and circumstance, as long as it is remembered that the ferret's well-being must be the most important consideration. There are obviously parameters that should be borne in mind when making the decision as to what type of cage one is to use for one's ferrets.

- Size
- Location/ positioning
- Materials and construction

Size
I do not like to state 'minimum' or 'recommended' sizes, since I believe that these become, all too quickly, the 'standard'. There can be no standard size for a ferret cage, since no two sets of circumstances will ever be identical. However, I understand that some guidance must be given.

Where one or two ferrets are kept in the same cage, a minimum size should be 1½ metres long, 1 metre high, and 1 metre deep, i.e. front to back (approximately 5 feet long, 3 feet high, and 3 feet deep). These sizes must, of course, be increased if more ferrets are housed in the cage.

If you are considering breeding from the ferrets in this cage, then at least one more cage must be provided, as it is not good practice to breed from a jill while she is in a communal cage.

Location/positioning
While ferrets can cope adequately with cold conditions, they are not necessarily happy in such conditions. Ferrets cannot cope with high temperatures, draughts or damp, and all of this should be considered when planning the location and positioning of the ferret's cage.

A stack of GRP (glass reinforced plastic) cages, used for holding breeding jills and their litters. Note water bottles on outside of each cage.

Some ferret keepers have their ferrets in the human home – a practice far more common in the United States than here in the UK. Within the human home, there will be some places better suited to housing ferrets than others, and one must examine closely the areas considered, remembering that the ferrets in that cage will be there for all the time when you are not at home to allow them free access. I do not believe that it is safe to allow ferrets constant free access to the human home; it is an accident waiting to happen.

The human home changes throughout the day, throughout the week, and throughout the year. In cold weather, we have central heating switching on early in a morning, switching off after we have left for work, and then repeating the sequence for our evenings at home. Once we have retired to bed, the house will cool rapidly, while we snuggle under our duvet to keep warm. If ferrets are kept in such an environment, they must be allowed to thermo-regulate, and their cage should not be placed anywhere where there is a possibility of over-heating or becoming chilled. Avoid placing cages near radiators or windows for these reasons. Within the cage, the ferrets must also be supplied with sufficient bedding material to allow them to adjust their temperatures, to maintain their comfort and their well-being.

Where ferrets are kept outside, similar considerations have to be made. Ferrets' cages must not be placed in an area where the cage will be subjected to the full heat of the midday sun, and neither must it be in an area swept by cold winds. In addition, it must be made waterproof (see next section), if the inhabitants are to be comfortable and healthy.

Take into account the prevailing winds in your locale, and ensure that the back of the ferret's cage faces in that direction, or that some form of windbreak or shelter is provided to prevent wind chill. Although they cannot tolerate high temperatures, ferrets do appreciate a little time to 'soak up the rays' and bask in the gentle warmth of early morning sunshine and, if possible, the cage should be positioned to allow for this.

The position of the cage must also take into account the human(s) who will need to visit the cage, on a regular basis, and service the cage and its inmates. A long walk through trees and across grass may be extremely pleasant in the summer months, but will take on a whole new perspective in the depths of winter.

Where I live, we regularly get large falls of snow and sub-zero temperatures for over three months of every year.

A path made of paving stones, concrete or even pebbles, will help prevent the human carers having to plough through acres of mud to get to the ferret cage. Likewise, the ferret cage itself should be placed on some form of hard standing; this will also help the task of keeping the area clean.

Materials and Construction

The materials used in the construction of any ferret cage will depend on the location of the finished product. Whereas cages destined to be kept inside a building will not need to be weather-proof, those kept outside certainly will.

Undoubtedly the most common material for the average do-it-yourself enthusiast is wood. This material is easy to work with, relatively cheap, and easily available. It is not waterproof, but can be made so by the application of paints and similar materials. When building in wood, ensure that the timber used is of sufficient thickness and quality. Plywood is probably the most commonly used type of timber, and this should be the type designed for outdoor use, or 'marine quality plywood'. Even if the cage is not intended for use outdoors, it is false economy to use anything less robust than this. Wood of 9 mm or 12 mm is good for most applications.

Any paint used must be non-toxic and 100 per cent 'animal safe'. Even though ferrets do not chew wood, they could still ingest paint etc., dislodged by the ferret's everyday activities.

Many commercial cages are manufactured from plastic, glass-reinforced plastic ('grp' or 'fibreglass') or similar substances. These are perfectly suitable for indoor use, but are not robust enough for outdoor usage. If dropped, these materials tend to crack, break or shatter, and so care must be taken when cleaning these cages. It is also worthwhile checking that detergents, disinfectants and other chemicals used for cleaning are safe on a particular piece of material, before using such substances.

Temperature Regulation

It is important that the room/building in which the ferret cages are kept has some form of temperature control, particularly in areas where temperatures can vary from very high to very low. Temperature regulation can be achieved by simply opening doors and windows to allow a flow of air, which in itself will allow warm air out of, and cooler air into, the building. Such air flow can easily be boosted by using electric fans, if a greater air flow is required. Conversely, in colder weather, windows and doors can be kept closed, and draught-excluding fittings can be used around all openings. However, care needs to be exercised so that, while draughts are eliminated, the building is still ventilated; without adequate ventilation, there is a distinct risk of a build-up of dust particles, along with debris from bedding and substrates, and this can easily lead to chest infections and/or breathing problems within the ferret population of the building.

Heaters, necessary in some areas in the colder weather, need to be selected and used with great care. Never use any heater with an open flame, as the risk of fire with such an appliance is far too great. Even where the flames are shielded from contact with flammable material, the carbon dioxide and carbon monoxide produced by burning fuels can be harmful to the animals in the building, as well as humans using the building. No heater should be placed directly under a cage, nor anywhere that debris – bedding, substrate etc. – may fall on to the heater.

We use oil-filled radiators, convection heaters and storage heaters in our buildings to keep the ambient temperature at about 22°C. In summer we use a series of electric fans to move air through the buildings, again attempting to keep the ambient temperature at about 22°C. Both our heaters and our fans are operated automatically, using thermostats. Any such wiring must always be installed by qualified electricians. As accidents can happen at any time, we also keep several fire extinguishers and a comprehensive first aid kit in each building/room.

Types of Cage

Traditionally, there are two types of cage for ferrets – cubs or courts. Cubs are simply 'hutches', while courts resemble aviaries, being a free-standing building into which humans can walk, while still standing. Here at the National Ferret School, we use both cubs and courts.

To help ensure security, we fit heavy duty hasps and staples on each cub, and use the very best padlocks on the courts outside our buildings; there is always someone who will covet your possessions, and it is only common sense to take precautions to help prevent the theft of your ferrets. The cubs are raised off the ground by the addition of legs; this helps reduce temperature loss by cold striking up from the cold, damp ground, and also puts the cub at a convenient height for you to work on, when cleaning and performing other maintenance duties.

Rather than waste the space below the cub, it is possible to turn it into an exercise area for the ferrets. This is easily achieved by covering the back and both sides of the area between the legs with weld mesh, and putting an opening door on the front; the addition of a solid timber floor will complete the exercise area. The ferrets can gain access to this exercise area via a length of corrugated piping, such as that sold for draining soil. By providing a shutter that can seal off the access, along with a separate nest box that can be placed in the bottom area, you will also have made a separate cub, for emergency use, or to separate ferrets in the breeding season.

While some ferret keepers make the entire cub floor from wire mesh, I have never held with this practice, and feel that it serves no useful purpose for the ferret's welfare. The only possible benefit is to the idle keeper, who will not have to concern himself with cleaning the cub as often as he should, as most of the inmate's faeces will fall through the mesh, although much will also adhere to the mesh itself, causing much work to remove. A solid wire floor will allow cold and draughts in to the cub, thereby making the occupants suffer. If owners cannot be bothered to keep the floors of their ferrets' cubs reasonably clean and dry, then I would question whether they should be keeping ferrets at all.

To ensure that one corner of the cub does not sink in to the ground, causing the cub to topple over, and that all debris from the cub is easily cleaned up, the area that the cubs stand on should be of either concrete or well laid paving slabs. It is also worth investing in a proper path to the cub area, again made of either concrete or paving slabs; the benefits of this will be realised during the bad weather, when the rain and snow will turn any other type of well-used path into a sea of mud.

At the National Ferret School, during the autumn and winter, we keep all of our ferrets in courts. These courts are 2 metres high,

4 metres long and 3 metres wide (approximately 7 feet x 13 feet x 10 feet). They have solid (concrete) floors, and solid (blocks) walls to about 500 mm (18 in), and then heavy gauge weld mesh to the top. The roofs are covered with corrugated steel, painted to prevent rust, and also as a means of insulation. The backs of the courts face the prevailing wind and are, therefore, made of solid blocks, in order to provide shelter for the inhabitants.

When spring arrives, and the hobs become restless and aggressive towards each other, with the onset of the breeding season, we move the hobs into cubs, which are inside buildings. Our cubs are 1½ metres x 1 metre x 1 metre high (approximately 5 feet x 3 feet x 3 feet). The hobs are kept one to a cub. As the jills come into season, they are removed from the courts and placed with the selected hob or hoblet (vasectomised male), where they are left for no more than twenty-four hours. After this time, the jills are removed, and those which have been mated with a normal hob, and are therefore (hopefully) pregnant, are placed into a cub of their own. They will remain in the cub until their kits have been born, and reached eight weeks of age. At this time, the kits and the jill are placed in a court with other similar ferrets. Jills mated with a hoblet are returned to the courts from which they were moved, until they come in season again. As all of our ferrets are marked with an electronic device (a microchip), identification is simple, and comprehensive record keeping ensures that no mistakes are made.

We also use some commercially produced cages, designed for laboratory or professional breeders. These are made of high impact fibreglass, and come in banks of three cages, all one above the other. They have a stainless steel front (bars), and the top and bottom are separate, kept in place by the racking into which they slide, rather like drawers. We use these for our stud males, and as 'honeymoon suites'. They are incredibly easy to clean and maintain, very light, and as the racking is on wheels, easy to move around the buildings; this helps ensure that wood shavings and other debris do not accumulate under the cages.

Courts are, in the author's opinion, the best general housing for ferrets, having many advantages over smaller cages:

- Space for the ferrets to exercise and play
- Space for the ferrets to find cool areas during times of high ambient temperatures

- Space for several ferrets to be kept together, while still allowing sufficient space for each ferret to get some privacy
- Easy access to humans to allow the servicing, repair and general maintenance of the cage

In order to give the ferrets a good environment, we cover the floor area with barley straw, and place rocks, tubes and tree stumps around the area. We also place several large, strong branches that stretch from the floor to the top of the court. Ferrets love to climb – if given the opportunity.

For ferrets kept inside the home, there is little need to make elaborate and totally weatherproof cages. Indeed, some owners simply leave their ferrets free to wander around the human home, with perhaps a pet bed or nest box in a corner, and a cat litter tray where the animals can relieve themselves. To many indoor ferret keepers, however, this is not sufficient; there are, after all, inherent dangers in allowing ferrets the run of the human home. Human feet, especially when encased in heavy shoes or boots, do nothing for the well-being of ferrets, while the animals themselves may climb into danger areas, or even push toes into electric appliances, sockets etc.

If your ferrets are to be allowed total free access to all parts of your home, you must take precautions to prevent injuries. These precautions include informing all visitors that ferrets are loose in the home, and ensuring that all cupboards, drawers etc. are kept closed. It is also advisable to keep all outside doors and windows closed too; they can act as avenues of escape for the ferrets, but may also allow access to cats or other potential predators.

Minimum housing for this type of ferret keeping is a cat or dog bed and a litter tray, preferably in each room to which the ferrets have access. As an absolute minimum, a bed and a litter tray should be provided on each level of the human home to which ferrets have access. Better still, is to provide a secure cage into which the ferret may be fastened as and when required, and to use it to keep the animals safe and secure when they cannot be attended to by you or your family. This cage need not be elaborate or even heavy duty, since it will only act as a temporary holding cage, for example when you have guests, or in hot weather when the house's windows and doors may well be left open. Nevertheless, the cage should be secure, and have an adequate supply of bedding, food and water available to the ferrets at all times.

To help reduce the amount of time and effort needed to keep the ferrets' environment safe and free from disease, we use removable litter trays (see Chapter 4).

Nest Boxes

We do not believe that it is always essential to give ferrets a separate sleeping compartment, but where the cage is exposed to strong winds and/or very low temperatures, such a nest box is useful. The biggest problem with nest boxes is that they tend to be prone to condensation. Because of this, we do not give wooden 'boxes' as sleeping quarters for our non-breeding adult ferrets; we use barrels as nest boxes. These barrels can be wooden or plastic, and some are sawn in half long ways, while others simply have one end removed, and a large (150 mm or 6 in) hole cut in what will be the top, when the barrel is laid on its side. Whichever design we use, the barrels are placed on trestles or bricks, to raise them off the floor, and thus away from draughts, and positioned in a sheltered part of the court; they are filled with top quality hay or barley straw. A further quantity of hay or straw is put on the floor under the trestles; this allows the ferrets to adjust the amount of bedding in their bed, or if we get a warm spell, to simply sleep under the barrels. Having kept ferrets in this way for over thirty years, in places where the ambient temperature regularly gets down to -10° C or lower, we have never had any problems with our ferrets in cold conditions. I have heard reports of ferrets that are kept in hay suffering from problems with seeds and/or dust, but in all the time I have kept ferrets, I have never had any such problem. We supply a number of nest boxes in every court, but do not use them in the cubs, except for breeding jills.

For pregnant jills, however, we feel that a well designed and constructed nest box is essential, for the benefit of both jill and litter. We give all of our pregnant jills nest boxes (one per cage), measuring approximately 230 mm wide x 240 mm high x 350 mm long (9 in x 9½ in x 14 in); we feel that this gives the jill a feeling of privacy and security, while at the same time helping maintain the kits in the nest, in a warm draught-free environment. The nest boxes are made from marine quality plywood, approx 12 mm (½ in) thick; to minimise condensation, we drill a series of holes along the top of each long side, and towards the end of one of the long sides, we cut an entrance hole about 50 mm (2 in) from one end, and about 90 mm (3½ in) from the floor of the nest box. The edges of this entrance hole are extremely smooth, in order to ensure that the jill's nipples and teats are not abraded; the entrance hole is about 100 mm (4 in) in diameter.

In the nest boxes, we lay a substrate of wood shavings, and on top of these add a large amount of soft barley straw; some jills make quite elaborate nests, while others simply lie on the straw. By supplying a quantity in excess of the jill's requirements, one gives the jill the opportunity to thermo-regulate the nest, by the simple movement – addition or removal – of the straw bedding. Some breeders use shredded paper; we find that this material becomes sodden very quickly, and has been known to form large, almost indestructible clumps on the legs and feet of kits, and on the nipples and teats of the jills. Sawdust must never be used, as this fine material can cause severe breathing problems in both kits and adult ferrets.

Any cage in which pregnant jills are kept, must have no opening larger than 25 mm x 25 mm (1 in x 1 in), otherwise kits close to weaning age may escape through them.

Cleaning Cages

We have tried a variety of materials and implements to clean the ferret cages over the years. The most important item is, without doubt, a good quality scraper. For the floor of the cages, we use the type sold in hardware stores for scraping wallpaper from walls; for the corners, we use the scrapers sold for removing paint. These are triangular in shape, and have a handle at right angles to the scraping blade.

Food Dishes and Water Bottles

Water is essential for all animals, and ferret owners should always make provision on the outside of the cub or court to attach a water bottle. This bottle should be of the gravity-feed type, complete with a stainless steel tube and nipple, and is far preferable to the traditional dish. Dishes can easily be tipped up – even quite

Where large numbers of ferrets are kept in a court, a poultry drinker provides the best solution.

heavy ones – and the water may soon become fouled and undrink-able, even if the dish is emptied, cleaned and replenished daily. It is also possible for young kits to fall into bowls of water and either drown or become seriously chilled. The tube to the bottle must be checked daily, in case it has become blocked. To help inhibit the growth of algae on the inside of the bottle (which is both unsightly and a health risk), a coloured bottle, such as a wine bottle, can be used.

Owing to the large numbers of ferrets kept here at the National Ferret School, we use an automatic watering system (see page 53).

Disinfectants

The cleaning of a ferret cage and its accessories is important and, to do the job correctly, a top quality disinfectant must be used. Not all disinfectants are suitable for use in ferret cages; indeed, some disinfectants can have serious deleterious effects on the ferrets.

Avoid all phenol-based disinfectants, as these are toxic to ferrets. Such disinfectants can enter the ferret's body through its skin, particularly the soles of its feet, and so even small quantities left on the surface of the cage's walls, or in the feed dishes or water bottles, can lead to the death of the ferret. Phenolic disinfectants are easy to detect; when mixed with water, they turn white.

Specialist disinfectants are available for a wide range of applications; some are designed to protect against specific pathogens, while others are designed to protect certain species against general threats. It is, therefore, possible to buy disinfectant that will protect reptiles, or will protect most species against *Streptococcus spp*. If in doubt about the efficacy and/or safeness of a particular disinfectant, consult a veterinary surgeon.

Whichever disinfectant you choose, ensure you use the correct dilution, that all surfaces, implements, dishes, bottles etc. are left in contact with the disinfectant for the correct amount of time (details will be on the label of the disinfectant container), and that the items are rinsed thoroughly before use.

Basics

The over-riding principle of genetics is that every living organism will receive 50 per cent of its inherited (genetic) material from *each* parent, via the nuclei of the germ cells (the male sperm and the female ova or egg). There are cases when this does not appear to be true, as some of the inherited traits from one parent may not be visible. However, the material *is* there, even though we cannot see all of it.

DNA

DNA (deoxyribonucleic acid) is made up of nucleic acids containing a form of sugar (deoxyribose), consisting of complex molecules. DNA is present in the chromosomes of all animal (and plant) cells, and carries encoded instructions for passing on hereditary characteristics. The DNA molecule itself is in the shape of a double helix, which resembles a spiral staircase. The rails of the staircase are made of alternating units of phosphate and the sugar deoxyribose; the treads are each composed of a pair of nitrogen-containing nucleotides.

The team who 'discovered' and described the structure of DNA was comprised of Francis Crick, Rosalind Franklin, Linus Pauling, James Watson and Maurice Wilkins. However, it was Watson and Crick who first published their paper (on 18 March 1953), and in 1962 Watson, Crick and Wilkins received the Nobel Prize for their work.

Some Historical Ideas

Some authorities insist that the sire (male) is more important than the dam (female), and that his genes will always 'overpower' the dam's. This is untrue. In his *Historia Animalium*, Aristotle stated that it was the father of an animal who provided the 'pattern' for the unborn offspring; the baby's mother merely provided the sustenance for the child, while it was in her womb and after the birth. Despite this theory being refuted by Mendel, many breeders still hold this as true, particularly so in the horse racing community.

It is also believed by some that it is the mother who determines the sex of the offspring. When Aristotle was questioned on this – it appeared to be totally contrary to his assertion that the offspring would be in their father's image, and yet many weren't, as they were of the opposite sex – he offered his opinion that this was simply due to what he termed as 'interference' from the mother. His belief was that, while in the womb, the dam could exert some kind of influence over the unborn child; this could range from the colour of the newborn's hair, to its gender. He also stated that, where a child was born deformed or disabled in any way, this too was the fault of the mother. The English king, Henry VIII, was obviously of this belief, as he kept changing wives because 'they were incapable of producing sons'. Not true. Another Greek, Hippocrates, believed that the result of a mating was due to the 'blending' of the characteristics of both parents, in a similar way to that of blending different watercolour paints. Again, not true.

One more theory that I must lay to rest here is that of newborn animals inheriting some or all of the 'acquired' characteristics of their parent(s). In other words, where a man is an accomplished athlete, able to run a record time in the marathon, all of his children, without the need for training, would also be able to do this. This, again, is patently not true.

Technical Terms

As in all activities, there is a certain amount of technical jargon that it is necessary to understand and this is true in genetics. In order to understand and therefore use genetics, you really do have to be able to both 'talk the talk' and 'walk the walk'. The physical appearance of a living being is referred to as its *phenotype*, while its genetic make-up is known as its *genotype*. It is obviously fairly simple to recognise a phenotype, but the genotype is hidden from us, although in many animals the phenotype gives a good indication of the animal's genotype. It is true to say that, for most ferret breeders, the main genetically inherited trait with which breeders are interested is the *pelage*, or coat colour.

Mendel referred to *genes* as units of inheritance, which I believe is a good description. He termed some of these genes as 'strong' and others as 'weak', or more correctly as *dominant* and *recessive*.

Where the animal's phenotype shows the result of recessive genes, then that animal has inherited two of these recessive genes (one from each parent); this animal is referred to as *homozygous*, a *zygote* being a fertilised ovum (egg). Recessive genes will only show in homozygous animals. Where the animal has inherited one dominant and one recessive gene, it is referred to as *heterozygous* or *split*, and only the dominant gene will show. Where an animal inherits two different recessive genes, e.g. for its coat colour, then neither of these will show in the animal's phenotype, but instead the ferret's coat colour will revert to its wild type phenotype – in the ferret, this is an animal with 'polecat' or fitchet markings. The total amount of genes present in any breeding programme or population is called the *gene pool*, and every effort should be made to maintain all of the genes in the gene pool.

Where a gene can cause harmful effects, it is termed *deleterious*. As mentioned earlier, we do not yet have details of the ferret's *genome* (i.e. the entire collection of genes carried by the species) and, although many breeders, particularly in the United States, have made assertions that there are some deleterious genes in the ferret, we do not – yet – know what they are. In the Syrian hamster (*Mesocricetus auratus*), a gene which may be described as deleterious is the anophthalmic white gene (Wh), a dominant gene. In the hamster, when combined with the gene for normal, or agouti, coloration (i.e. the heterozygote Whwh), the Wh gene produces an animal that has a back (top) of agouti, with a pure white stomach, rather than the creamy coloration that one would normally expect in the golden hamster. In addition, the guard hairs of the hamster are white, giving the animal a 'frosted' appearance; its eyes are ruby red. However, when two hamsters, both of whom are carrying the Wh gene, are mated, it can be expected that 50 per cent of the litter will inherit the Wh gene from each parent, creating the homozygote (WhWh); this is a pure white animal. In this case, these animals will be born with, at best, rudimentary eyes (*microphthalmic*) or no eyes whatsoever (*anophthalmic*). While both of these traits are, of course, undesirable, it should be noted that where only one of the parents carries the Wh gene, the resultant offspring will be heterozygous or split for this gene, and will therefore have the genotype Whwh; in this case the eyes are perfectly normal. While some would argue that no animal carrying such a gene should ever be produced, it should also be remembered that, where a deleterious gene is combined with other genes, the results can sometimes be quite spectacular, as in the example given earlier. In this example, a normal (agouti) Syrian hamster mated with a hamster genotype Whwh, will produce 25 per cent of its litter that are heterozygous for Wh (i.e. Whwh), and of the coloration mentioned earlier. Where the animal is to be used for exhibition, and only bred by knowledgeable breeders, this is acceptable to most people; the potential problems may occur when such animals are released into the 'pet market' and bred haphazardly by inexperienced breeders, who are likely to produce many eyeless hamsters.

Meiosis is the process of reduction division, whereby the normal complement of chromosomes in the cell is reduced to half; it occurs in the specialised tissues of the *testes* and *ovary*, and leads to the production of *gametes*. These cells are referred to as *haploid* gametes and spores, and consist of a single duplication of the genetic material followed by two mitotic divisions.

Where offspring are produced from parents who differ in only one trait, this is referred to as *monohybrid inheritance*. Where the

The head of a hob should be big and broad.

parents differ in two traits, this is known as *di-hybrid inheritance,* and where the parents differ in more than two traits, as *multi-hybrid inheritance.*

Sexual dimorphism is the term used to describe the physical differences between the genders of the same species; in ferrets, this manifests itself in the hob having the potential to be bigger and broader than the jill. *Sex-linked traits* are those traits whose genes are located on the sex chromosome of the ferret, and so occur exclusively, or predominantly, in one sex only. In cats, Syrian hamsters (*Mesocricetus auratus*) and other species, tortoiseshell markings are found only on female animals. These characteristics are recessive and are determined by genes on the X chromosome; all female animals possess two X chromosomes, whereas males have one X chromosome and one Y chromosome

The exchange of genetic material between members of a homologous chromosome pair is known as *crossing-over,* and occurs during synapsis. Gene interaction is where several genes collaborate to produce one phenotypic characteristic, such as in the albino ferret, where the eyes are clear (although appearing pinkish).

One of a pair, or series, of genes similarly located on homologous chromosomes is known as an *allele.* These alleles occupy the same position, known as the *locus,* (plural *loci*) on homologous chromosomes, and are separated from each other during meiosis.

Where two alleles, or genes, for a specific trait are equally strong, a mixture of the two phenotypes can result. This is known as *co-dominance.*

The gender of a ferret is determined by the combination of two chromosomes – X and Y. As mentioned above, the male has an XY, while the female has an XX. There is obviously a 50:50 chance of producing a jill or a hob, as illustrated in the Punnett square below:

	X	X
X	XX	XX
Y	XY	XY

In addition, the X chromosome differs from the Y chromosome in size; the X gene is a medium-sized chromosome, while the Y chromosome is a small one. Obviously, then, the X chromosome is capable of carrying far more genetic information (i.e. genes) than the Y chromosome.

Where a genetic factor is responsible for the premature death of an organism, this is called a *lethal factor*. Some genes can cause the death of the foetus, while it is in the womb, whereas others will lead to a premature death. Some lethal genes are sex-linked, i.e. linked to the X or Y genes, and so only affect one gender, e.g. haemophilia in humans. This is carried by females, but only manifests itself in males.

Epistasis is the term used to describe the interaction between non-allelic genes in which one gene has a dominant effect on the expression of the other, whereas the result of the interaction of several genes is known as *polygenic*.

The checkerboard-like arrangement used for determining the results of a mating involving at least two differing genes, is known as a *Punnett square*; this was named after its inventor, Reginald Crundall Punnett (see page 83). Its use is fairly straightforward; refer to the later examples of mono-hybrid and di-hybrid inheritance.

Gregor Mendel

Gregor Johann Mendel, an Austrian monk and amateur biologist, carried out work on what we now call genetics, and this work was published in 1866. Mendel's work on heredity has now become the basis of the modern theory of genetics. Born on 22 July 1822 in Heizendorf, Austria (now Hyncice, in the Czech Republic), to a poor farming family, Mendel escaped his life of poverty by entering the monastery of the Augustinian Order of St Thomas, at Brunn in Moravis (now Brno in the Czech Republic). The Brunn monastery was a teaching order with an excellent reputation as a centre of learning and scientific enquiry.

Mendel attended the University of Vienna, studying for a teaching diploma, but did not impress the university staff, who did not consider him to be capable of his studies. In fact, in a report from one of his university examiners, Mendel was described as 'lacking insight and the requisite clarity of knowledge'. Mendel returned to the monastery in 1853 as a failure.

While studying in Vienna, Mendel had met a biologist called

Frank Unger. Unger exhibited a practical view of inheritance, free from spiritual and church influences, and this appealed to Mendel, probably owing to his own farming background. Unger's influence was so great that Mendel decided to stay on at the monastery and use his time to carry out practical experiments in biology, even though the bishop had previously refused to allow the monks to even teach biology. Mendel succeeded in obtaining permission from the bishop, and began his investigation into variation, heredity and evolution in plants, studying the common garden pea, *Pisum*, which grew in the monastery garden.

Mendel cultivated and tested at least 28,000 pea plants between 1856 and 1863. He carefully analysed traits for comparison – shape of seed, colour of seed, tall stemmed and short stemmed, tall plants and short plants. He self-pollinated and wrapped each individual plant to prevent accidental pollination by insects, and collected the seeds produced by the plants. Mendel studied the offspring of these seeds, and noted that some plants bred 'true' while others did not. He also discovered that, by crossing tall and short parent plants he got hybrid offspring that resembled the tall parent rather than being plants of a 'medium' (i.e. in between) height. From these results, Mendel conceived the concept of 'units of inheritance', which we now refer to as genes. He observed that these units could either express 'strong' (dominant or a trait that shows up in an offspring) or 'weak' (recessive or a trait masked or hidden by a dominant gene) characteristics, and he worked out the pattern of inheritance of these traits, producing two general 'rules' that became known as 'Mendel's laws of heredity'. In 1866 Mendel published his work on heredity in the *Journal of the Brno Natural History Society*, but received no recognition for his work, probably because it was not understood by the influential people in his field. In 1868, Mendel was elected Abbot of the monastery and his work on genetics remained unrecognised for over thirty years.

When Mendel died in 1884 aged sixty-two, the new Abbot of the monastery burned many of Mendel's papers, and it was not until 1900 that his work was recognised by three independent investigators, including the Dutch botanist, Hugo De Vries. However, it was not until the early twentieth century that the full significance of Mendel's work was recognised when, as a result of years of research in population genetics, investigators were able to demonstrate that the Darwinian theory of evolution could be described in terms of the change in gene frequency of Mendelian pairs of characteristics in a population over successive generations. Modern genetics had, at last, been born.

It was Reginald Crundall Punnett who brought the work of Gregor Mendel to scientific notice in a way in which the scientists would take the matter seriously. Punnett graduated from Caius College, Cambridge, in 1898, with a first class degree in Natural Sciences, specialising in zoology. Punnett was a believer in Mendel's theories, and wrote the first textbook on the subject. Between 1904 and 1910, Punnett, working with William Bateson, confirmed Mendel's theories experimentally. The experiments conducted by Punnett and Bateson mainly involved poultry and sweet green peas, and their experiments proved Mendel's explanations of sex determination, sex linkage, complimentary factors, factor integration and autosomal linkage.

During the First World War, Punnett developed a technique of separating male and female chicks using sex-linked plumage colours, creating the first auto-sexing breed of poultry, the Cambar chicken. He was a founding member of the Genetics Society and helped produce the *Journal of Genetics*. Punnett was also the inventor of the Punnett square, which is still used widely in genetics, to depict the number and variety of genetic combinations (see later in this chapter).

In simple terms, Mendel discovered that there are two genes for every characteristic of any living thing; it is important to remember that, although Mendel's work was carried out on plants, the principles apply to animals and all other living organisms on this planet, also. The gametes of the plant or animal can contain only one gene for each characteristic, and the paternal and maternal genes occur in the same ratio among the gametes. The latter principle (i.e. the manner in which genes are evenly divided during the formation of gametes), is known as Mendel's First Law, which is also known as the 'law of segregation'.

Properly, Mendel's First Law is stated thus:

> The two members of a gene pair (alleles) segregate (separate) from each other in the formation of gametes. Half the gametes carry one allele, and the other half carries the other allele.

Mendel's Second Law is sometimes referred to as the 'law of independent assortment'. This states that differing traits are inherited independently of each other; this, however, applies only to genes on different chromosomes. Mendel's experiments had proved that, where he crossed a tall (dominant) pea plant with a dwarf (recessive) plant, some of each of which had purple (dominant) flowers, and others white (recessive) flowers, the resultant 'offspring', known as the F1 generation, would all show the dominant for each characteristic, i.e. they would all be tall with purple flowers, while the next (F2) generation would produce every possible combination of these characteristics. This, argued Mendel, could only happen if the genes were independent of each other, and not 'linked' simply because of the fact that they had been inherited together from the same strain. Below is an example, set out in two Punnett squares.

As we do not (yet) have accurate details of the ferret's genome, we will use as our premise a cross between a pair of rabbits, one of which is black with long ears, while the other is white with short ears. Black is dominant, and is given the symbol A, while white is recessive, and so given the symbol a. Long ears are dominant, and represented by the symbol Z, while short ears are recessive, and thus allotted the symbol z. In genetic shorthand, a mating (or cross) between two animals is denoted by an x (see below).

Di-hybrid Inheritance
We will therefore have the following example of di-hybrid inheritance:

Black, long-eared (AAZZ) x white, short-eared (aazz)

This would be set out in the Punnett square as:

	AZ	AZ	AZ	AZ
az	AaZz	AaZz	AaZz	AaZz
az	AaZz	AaZz	AaZz	AaZz
az	AaZz	AaZz	AaZz	AaZz
az	AaZz	AaZz	AaZz	AaZz

All of the F1 generation (i.e. those inside the Punnett square) have the genotype AaZz, and so have the phenotype of black with long ears, i.e. *only* the dominant traits show, even though all of the F1 generation are carrying the recessive genes for both white and short ears.

If we were to carry out sibling matings of the F1 generation, i.e. mate genotype AaZz with genotype AaZz, then the following would result:

	AZ	Az	az	aZ
AZ	AAZZ	AAZz	AaZz	AaZZ
Az	AAZz	AAzz	Aazz	AaZz
az	AaZz	Aazz	aazz	aaZz
aZ	AaZZ	AaZz	aaZz	aaZZ

Remembering that, where a pairing shows only dominant, or both a dominant and a recessive gene for the same characteristic, the dominant trait *only* will show, the offspring would be:

Genotype	Phenotype
AAZZ	Black, long-eared
AAZz	Black, long-eared
AAzz	Black, short-eared
Aazz	Black, short-eared
AaZz	Black, long-eared
AaZZ	Black, long-eared
aazz	White, short-eared
aaZz	White, long-eared
aaZZ	White, long-eared

In this mating, there is every possible combination of the four alleles, i.e. sixteen. The most common (25 per cent) is the double heterozygote AaZz (the same genotype, and therefore phenotype, as the parents of this mating), with the phenotype black, long-eared. Only one of the sixteen (6.25 per cent) is the white, short-eared (aazz). This type of mating will always give the same ratio of results; of course the actual numbers depend on the size of the litter.

If we wished to increase the ratio of the white, short-eared rabbits in the F2 generation, then we would have mated the white, short-eared parent (aazz) with one of its offspring (AaZz), and this would give us the following:

	az	az	az	az
AZ	AaZz	AaZz	AaZz	AaZz
Az	Aazz	Aazz	Aazz	Aazz
az	aazz	aazz	aazz	aazz
aZ	aaZz	aaZz	aaZz	aaZz

This time, the F2 generation would produce the following:

Genotype	Phenotype
AaZz	Black, long-eared
Aazz	Black, short-eared
aazz	White, short-eared
aaZz	White, long-eared

As can be seen from these results, the parent/offspring mating would produce 25 per cent white, short-eared animals, almost four times as many as the sibling mating. In addition, it must be remembered that, as each animal has inherited 50 per cent of its genetic make-up from each parent, a wider number of differing genes will be passed on to the next generation when mating parent with offspring, than in a sibling mating. It is important to keep the gene pool as large as possible, and so the parent/offspring mating is always preferable to the sibling mating.

Although, as stated earlier, there are no recognised and identified genes in the ferret, the easiest example to give here involves the crossing of a 'pure' (i.e. homozygous) fitchet with an albino. The true albino gene is a recessive, and the phenotype of this animal is pure white (although the white may appear yellow in certain lights, at certain times of the year, and in some older ferrets) and so the genotype of this animal is always homozygous for albino. It should be noted here that, because of this homozygosity, albinos cannot carry any other gene for coat colour. The albino's eyes are clear, although they will appear pink, as the blood vessels in and behind the eyes colour the eyes.

In such a cross, all of the first generation (F1) would have the phenotype of their dark parent, but all would be heterozygous for albino. If one of the heterozygous offspring is mated back to its albino parent, then approximately 50 per cent of the litter should be albino. If siblings from the F1 generation are mated, then 25 per cent of the litter should be albino. Once again, it must be remembered that the percentages are theoretical, and the overall size of the litter will have an effect on these percentages, as well as the 'randomness' of chance. The latter can best be described as in the chance of tossing a coin, where there is a 50:50 chance of its landing on heads. If it is only tossed once, then the result cannot be 50:50. Even if tossed several more times, it is often possible to get results far from the theoretical expectation of 50:50. However, if one or both of the 'original' parents were carrying any recessive genes, then the results would differ, depending on which recessive genes were being carried.

In addition, genes sometimes 'go wrong' or mutate. When this happens, it can produce a whole range of differences, from having more or fewer limbs than normal, to producing a coat colour that has never been seen before. Such mutations must always be treated with caution, since any one of them could have deleterious effects on the offspring produced. Sometimes, the first one or two generations are seemingly OK, at least phenotypically, but later generations may well show the deleterious effects of the mutant gene.

The Loci

The letters used to denote genes are not simply plucked from the air, at least if selected by those who understand the subject. While some 'authorities' will use the lower case 'a' to denote an albino, the 'a' is derived from the mutation of the agouti gene. As the agouti is dominant, it is assigned the letter 'A' (note the use of upper case), and so the recessive mutant – black – is obviously assigned the lower case letter 'a'.

The main colours of all animals are controlled and determined by six loci. Each of these loci has at least one mutant allele, while some have several. The loci are as follows:

- A   The agouti
- B   Black pigment
- C   The albino series
- D   Dense pigment
- E   Extension series
- P   Pink-eyed dilute

Research has shown that there are three other loci worthy of consideration, having occurred in at least two species of small livestock, viz:

- U   Umbrous
- O   Sex-linked yellow
- Wh   Anophthalmic white

The Agouti

There are two loci influencing the agouti, or 'wild type' coat, and this is one. In livestock in general, there are two common mutants of this – the tan pattern, which gives an animal with a black back and white, yellow or tan stomach, and the non-agouti, which gives a self black.

Black Pigment

The mutant allele alternative to black is brown or chocolate. Although we do not know the details of the ferret, in most species, there is a single mutant, although in the cat and the mouse, there are two.

The Albino Series

This, the normal gene for full colour, or maximum pigmentation, has many mutants, with every known species having at least one. The most commonly known are albino, chinchilla and Himalayan.

Dense Pigment

This mutant allele causes a clumping of the pigment granules, giving a diluting effect, often known as 'blueing'.

Extension Series

This is the second loci concerned with agouti coat, and mutant alleles modify the colour by the over-production of black pigment, known as dominant black, and a patchwork of yellow and red.

Pink-eyed Dilute

This mutant allele causes the pigment granules to flocculate (or aggregate). This causes a diluting or even a 'silver-blueing' of the coat colour. The eyes appear pink or red, an effect not seen with the dense pigment; I believe that this gene may be one of those responsible for the so-called 'silver' ferret.

Umbrous

This is a dominant gene that produces an over abundance of black pigment. Although similar to dominant black, this gene is inherited independently of the extension alleles.

Sex-linked Yellow

This mutant allele produces a yellow or orange phenotype in male animals, while in females, it manifests itself as tortoiseshell.

Anophthalmic

A dominant gene, this produces animals with white coats and small, or non-existent, eyes in the homozygous, while in the heterozygous, the animal usually has ruby red eyes, with white spotting and/or brindling.

Coat Types

In animals in general, there are three main mutations affecting coat type – long hair, satin and rex (curly hair).

Practical Example

If a breeder crosses a hob fitchet with a jill fitchet, it is possible that not all of the offspring in the F1 generation will be fitchets. Often, even though the ferrets' owner(s) believes that both the hob and jill ferrets are homozygous, one or even both of the ferrets may be heterozygous for a recessive variety. If this is the case i.e. both parents carry the same hidden recessive genes, then one can expect some of the kits to show the recessive colour.

If, for example, both of the original parents are heterozygous for albino, then one can expect approximately 25 per cent of the F1 litter to be albino. If the same heterozygous (for albino) ferret was mated with an albino, then there would be an expectation of approximately 50 per cent of albinos in the F1 generation. It should be remembered that the albino gene is recessive, and therefore the albino cannot carry any other gene affecting coat colour. If one parent is heterozygous for albino, and the other parent heterozygous for another recessive coat colour, then one can expect all of the F1 generation to be fitchet, since there can be no possibility of a pair of the same recessive genes pairing.

If both parents are heterozygous for *two* recessive coat colour genes then, although both parents would have the phenotype of fitchet, any recessive colour will only manifest itself in a homozygote; where an animal carries two *different* recessive genes for coat colour it will revert to wild type, i.e. appear to be a fitchet. In this case the litter would be expected to consist of 25 per cent of each of the recessive colours and 50 per cent fitchets, with the fitchets being heterozygous for both recessive coat colours.

In order to illustrate this phenomenon, I will use an example from the Syrian hamster (*Mesocricetus auratus*). In this hamster, the gene for black is a, while the gene for cream is e; therefore, a black hamster will have the genotype aa, while a cream hamster will have the genotype ee. If we mate a black hamster with a cream, we will produce agouti, or 'golden' coloured hamsters, as illustrated below:

	e	e
a	ae	ae
a	ae	ae

As will, I hope, be accepted by now, recessive colours will only appear if they are homozygous. In this example, every animal produced is heterozygous, for both black and cream. Therefore, neither cream nor black will show; rather the animals will 'revert to wild type', i.e. have the wild phenotypes, which in this case is golden (agouti).

We now have three possible matings for the F2 generation, viz:

1 Sibling matings
2 Cream parent x offspring
3 Black parent x offspring

If we mate together siblings (i.e. ae x ae), the following Punnett square will illustrate the outcome:

	a	e
a	aa	ae
e	ae	ee

This time, the F2 generation would produce the following:

GENOTYPE	PHENOTYPE
aa	Black (25 per cent)
ee	Cream (25 per cent)
ae	Golden/agouti (50 per cent) – all heterozygous for both black and cream

If we mate the cream parent with one of its offspring, the following will take place:

	e	e
a	ae	ae
e	ee	ee

This time, the F2 generation would produce the following:

GENOTYPE	PHENOTYPE
ee	Cream (50 per cent)
ae	Golden/agouti (50 per cent) – all heterozygous for both black and cream

If we mate the black parent with one of its offspring, the following will take place:

	a	a
a	aa	aa
e	ae	ae

This time, the F2 generation would produce the following:

GENOTYPE	PHENOTYPE
aa	Black (50 per cent)
ae	Golden/agouti (50 per cent) – all heterozygous for both black and cream

If one were lucky enough to produce a new mutation coat colour/variety, then it is important that the gene(s) responsible for this, i.e. a mutant gene, is safeguarded. In other words, where a mutant variety is produced, every effort should be made to preserve that mutation. Sometimes only one member of a litter will exhibit the mutant coloration, and this can cause some problems for the novice breeder. After all, doesn't it need both a male and a female to produce more ferrets? However, with a little thought, it will be seen that, although both a male and a female are necessary for reproduction, it is not necessary that both of these animals are of the same variety.

The example below is based on a pairing of true homozygous fitchets, which have produced a mutant coat variety, which is phenotypically green (highly unlikely, but this will demonstrate the principles involved). For the sake of this example, I have designated the 'green' gene as g, and therefore the fitchet gene needs to be designated as G. In other words, the fitchets will have the genotype of GG, while the green ferret has the genotype of gg.

To produce more green ferrets, we will need to ensure that we can produce a pairing of g genes. While this obviously cannot be done in the F1 generation (since we only have the one ferret carrying the mutant gene), we can ensure that it should happen in the F2 generation, always remembering the principle of 'randomness', as described earlier, in the example of tossing two coins.

First Mating

	g	g
G	Gg	Gg
G	Gg	Gg

The F1 generation would produce the following:

GENOTYPE	PHENOTYPE
Gg	Fitchet

All of the F1 generation would, therefore, be phenotypically fitchet, but heterozygous for green.

We now have two choices to produce the F2 generation:

- Parent mated with offspring
- Sibling matings

If we were to use the original green parent, there would be a 50 per cent chance of the mutant – g – gene pairing with another g gene, while, if we used a sibling (i.e. sister x brother) mating, there would only be a 25 per cent chance of producing more green ferrets. It should also be borne in mind that we need to keep our gene pool as large as possible. The best way to do this, in this example, is to use the parent x offspring mating, since the parent will be carrying many more different genes than the offspring. To mate siblings would cause the gene pool to shrink, thus reducing the number of genes available to the breeding programme.

Second Mating

1)   Green parent x offspring

	g	g
G	Gg	Gg
g	gg	gg

In this example, the F2 generation would produce the following:

GENOTYPE	PHENOTYPE
Gg	Fitchet (50 per cent)
gg	Green (50 per cent)

All of the fitchets will be heterozygous for green. The green ferrets can only be homozygous for green, and so cannot carry any other gene affecting coat colour.

2) Sibling mating

	G	g
G	GG	Gg
g	Gg	gg

In this example, the F2 generation would produce the following:

GENOTYPE	PHENOTYPE
GG	Fitchet – homozygous (25 per cent)
Gg	Fitchet – heterozygous for green (50 per cent)
gg	Green – homozygous (25 per cent)

It is not possible to distinguish the homozygous fitchets from those heterozygous for green, since the phenotypes of both will be fitchet.

In each case, we should now have some ferrets that are phenotypically green and obviously, as the mutant gene is a recessive, all green ferrets are homozygous for green, and will not carry any other gene that can affect coat colour. While it is highly unlikely that green ferrets will ever be produced, the principles explained here can be used to 'fix' or maintain any recessive feature and/or gene.

Epistasis or the Masking of Genes

There are some instances when one or more genes may 'mask' the presence of other genes; this is often a source of confusion and frustration for those first approaching genetics. The concept of dominance can be easily accepted by most people, as it is usually the 'normal' gene that is dominant to the mutant gene. However, the principle of dominance can only be applied to the effects of pairs of genes on the same locus. Probably the best way to explain masking is by giving an example.

In all mammals, albinism is due to the recessive gene c; this is obviously a mutant allele of the C gene, i.e. the gene for normal pigmentation. The genotype for an albino is, therefore cc, and the reader would be forgiven for believing that this means that the albino cannot carry genes for any other colour. This is not necessarily the case, as the albino gene masks the presence of other genes.

Using the Syrian hamster as an example, if we were to mate an albino (AAcc) with a black (aaCC), all of the F1 generation would be genotypically AaCc, and so phenotypically agouti (wild type). The reason for this, although not obvious, is that, under its white coat, the albino is an agouti. The F1 generation is phenotypically agouti simply because the a and c alleles are recessive to the A and C genes. If we use the F1 generation to produce an F2 generation, the expected progeny will be as outlined in the Punnett square below.

Agouti (AaCc) x Agouti (AaCc)

	AC	aC	Ac	ac
AC	AACC	AaCC	AACc	AaCc
aC	AaCC	aaCC	AaCc	aaCc
Ac	AACc	AaCc	AAcc	Aacc
ac	AaCc	aaCc	Aacc	aacc

F2 Generation

AACC	Agouti (1)
AaCC	Agouti (2)
AACc	Agouti (2)
AaCc	Agouti (4)
aaCC	Black (1)
aaCc	Black (2)
AAcc	Albino (1)
Aacc	Albino (2)
aacc	Albino (1)

In other words the hamsters produced would be nine agouti, three black and four albino, or given as a ratio 9:3:4. However, as will be seen in the Punnett square, the genotypes AAcc, Aacc and aacc are phenotypically albino, although genotypically agouti or black. Why, then does the c allele mask the a or A genes? Albino animals, by definition, have a total lack of pigmentation and so, with no pigment to modify, neither the A nor the a genes can express themselves. In other words, albinos can mask all known colour genes.

There are more genes that mask the presence of other genes, including the e gene in cavies, and the O and the W genes in the cat. In all cases, the masking gene removes the means by which other genes produce their effect. The technical term for masking is epistasis and so, one could describe the c gene as epistatic to all other coloured genes, while the e gene is epistatic to a limited number of genes.

Chapter Seven

Planning and Establishing a Breeding Programme

Why Breed?

I believe that *every* breeding programme *must* have the goal of improving the animals in some way. To breed any animals without this objective is not, to my mind, justifiable.

Aims of Programme

Before embarking on any project, it is always wise to ask yourself why you are doing it, and what you wish to achieve; the breeding of any animals is a project that requires long and careful consider-ation, and must always be carried out for a valid reason. For most of us, that valid reason is the continuing quest for our elusive goal – the perfect ferret, whether it be for use as a pet, for working (hunting – 'rabbiting' or 'ferreting'), exhibition, business, sport (e.g. ferret racing), or for conservation purposes, as in the American black-footed ferret project.

When I started my 'ferret career', back in the mid 1960s, I was incredibly lucky in acquiring a trio of ferrets (one hob and two jills) that were of good breeding, excellent looks, were brilliant workers, and all had a superb temperament. However, within a couple of years, I was sure that there was scope (and to my mind a definite need) for improvement, which could only be achieved by carefully controlled selective breeding. I was using the ferrets for rabbiting, and had encountered a few problems that I associated with the size of the ferrets I was using; I considered them to be too large. My theory was – and still is – that if a ferret is too big, it cannot move quickly enough down the long and winding tunnels of a burrow. Worse still, if the rabbit runs into a 'stop' (a cul-de-sac), a large ferret can do nothing other than scratch away at the rabbit until the luckless coney is dead, by which time the ferret is tired and hungry, and will eat her fill from the cadaver before curling up and going to sleep, causing consternation for the humans waiting for her at the surface. To extract such a ferret from a 'lay up' entails digging out the animal – not easy in very hard, stony ground. Conversely, a ferret that is too small may well not have the physical resources to work for long enough periods to be of use, and may even be dragged around the burrow by a large rabbit into whom she manages to sink her teeth. I also have a great liking for really dark ferrets, and so I began to select my breeding stock for these traits, breeding only from those that most closely matched my criteria.

I decided that I would produce my own line of ferrets to my own exacting criteria – 'perfect' rabbiting ferrets. While I realised that this would take many years of hard work, careful planning, ruthless selection and, of course, lots of luck, I considered it to be worth the effort. I still do.

For reference, my criteria were, and still are:

- Excellent temperament
- Good workers
- Dark coloration
- Right size, i.e. small without being tiny
- No physical defects

Unfortunately, much of my work was lost when, in February 1994, thieves stole my entire collection of ferrets – forty-six animals in total. This was a devastating blow to me and my efforts, and I feared that I would never again have such excellent ferrets as I believed I had had at that time. Luckily, not all humans are as vile and despicable as those who stole my ferrets, and many breeders rallied to my aid. I was offered the offspring of animals I had bred and subsequently sold to other breeders and, in some cases, the very animals that I had bred and sold. Although not the ferrets I had lost – and no breeder passes on the very best of the animals they breed – they were certainly good ferrets. And so I began my quest again, and it continues to this day. Like so many other animal breeders, I have to admit to being a bit of a 'perfectionist', and I doubt I will ever produce the 'perfect' ferret in my lifetime, but I will have great fun, enjoyment and satisfaction attempting to do so.

You may not have such lofty and egotistic ideas as mine, but may simply want to have more ferrets like the ones that you now own, or you may wish to increase the number of ferrets you have without the need to buy any. Do not, however, make the mistake of believing that you can make large amounts of money from ferret breeding; unless you have huge numbers of ferrets, can sell all of them at a really good price, and operate a proper business, you will never make your fortune from such an undertaking.

It must also be said that, for many ferret owners, there is no real need to breed, since there are plenty of breeders of ferrets from whom new stock can easily be obtained. Unless you feel that you really do need to breed your own ferrets, it may well be easier, simpler and cheaper to buy new ferrets.

The Importance of Planning

If you decide to embark on a ferret-breeding project, you must spend time planning before starting the project. I find the best way to begin planning is to 'brain storm', starting at why you wish to breed, to what you will do with the end result, i.e. the kits produced by the breeding programme. To help make things easier, I use a piece of 'mind-mapping' software, and the following diagram has been produced using this. To my mind, such software makes life easier and planning more efficient.

The following headings will help explain the diagram; obviously the details of each heading will vary from breeder to breeder, and also from breeding programme to breeding programme. The brain storming exercise should be carried out every year for every breeding programme.

Goals/objectives
As stated previously, I believe that it is vital that one has clear objectives/goals for the breeding programme *before* commencing the project, and these objectives must be clear and achievable.

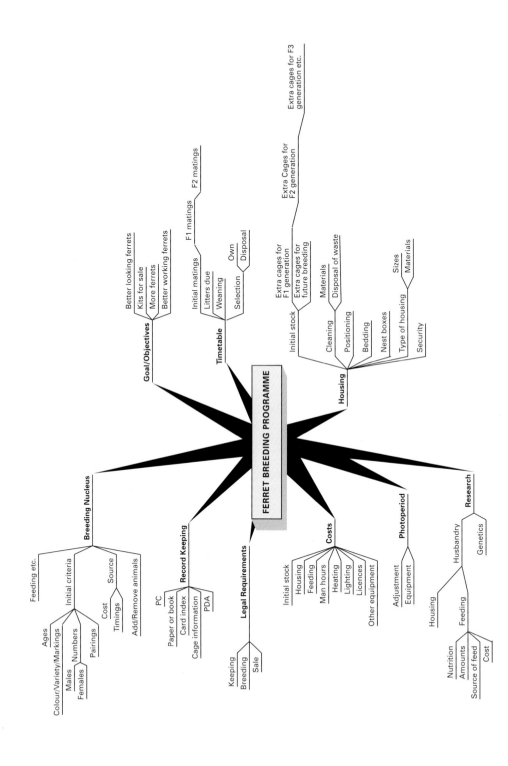

FERRET BREEDING PROGRAMME

Goal/Objectives
- Better looking ferrets
- Kits for sale
- More ferrets
- Better working ferrets

Timetable
- Initial matings
  - Litters due
  - Weaning
  - Selection
    - Own
    - Disposal
- F1 matings
- F2 matings

Housing
- Initial stock
- Extra cages for F1 generation
- Extra cages for future breeding
- Extra Cages for F2 generation
- Extra cages for F3 generation etc.
- Cleaning
  - Materials
  - Disposal of waste
- Positioning
- Bedding
- Nest boxes
- Type of housing
  - Sizes
  - Materials
- Security

Breeding Nucleus
- Feeding etc.
- Initial criteria
  - Colour/Variety/Markings
  - Ages
  - Males
  - Females
  - Numbers
  - Pairings
- Cost
- Timings
- Source
- Add/Remove animals

Record Keeping
- PC
- Paper or book
- Card index
- Cage information
- PDA

Legal Requirements
- Keeping
- Breeding
- Sale

Costs
- Initial stock
- Housing
- Feeding
- Man hours
- Heating
- Lighting
- Licences
- Other equipment

Photoperiod
- Adjustment
- Equipment

Research
- Husbandry
  - Housing
  - Feeding
    - Nutrition
    - Amounts
    - Source of feed
    - Cost
- Genetics

Breeding Nucleus
The choice of the animals to make up the original breeding stock must be given much thought. The animals chosen must be as near to your idea of the 'perfect' ferret as possible, in order to make the goal of the breeding programme achievable. You must have a reasonable number of animals, and a suitable sex ratio. I would not dream of operating any breeding programme without a minimum of six jills and three hobs. The relationship of these animals must also be considered carefully, since too much inbreeding may result in *inbreeding depression*, resulting in smaller litters and also a general decline in the condition of the progeny of such matings.

When sourcing the initial breeding stock, care should be taken to obtain animals with not only the correct phenotype (physical appearance), but also the correct genotype (genetic make-up). Unless this is done, the progeny of the litters produced in the breeding programme will be totally unpredictable. The ferrets should also be in excellent health, have a superb temperament, and be extremely fit. If the progeny of the breeding programme is intended for work or sport, the initial breeding nucleus must also have the necessary attributes.

Legal Requirements
In some areas, laws exist that can have a serious effect on any breeding plans you may have. In some areas, the keeping of ferrets is banned, while in others, to sell ferrets will require one or more licences. Some local, regional or national authorities have restrictions on the disposal of 'animal waste', while others impose restrictions on how many animals can be kept at any one location. Utility suppliers (water, gas and electricity) also have differing rules; some insist that, where a business – no matter how small – is established, a different (usually higher) rate is charged. In the UK, VAT (value added tax) is charged on all fuels supplied for businesses. It is imperative that legal advice is sought before embarking on any breeding programme.

Costs
As in all endeavours, costs will be incurred throughout the project, and these costs should be estimated before embarking on the scheme. Costs will be incurred for (among other items) the initial

breeding stock, cages, food, water bottle/dishes etc., vet fees, licences, heating and lighting equipment, heating and lighting fuel bills, substrates, bedding and the disposal of these, PCs and other such equipment.

Photoperiod
If it is wished to breed the ferrets at a particular time of year, or even throughout the year, then considerations must be given to the manipulation of photoperiod to allow this. Lighting, timing devices and other equipment will be needed for this.

Research
The military adage that 'time spent in reconnaissance is never wasted' can be applied to projects of this nature. One should thoroughly research the venture if success is to be achieved. The research should include such items as the natural history of ferrets, husbandry, genetics, housing, nutrition and feeding.

Timetable
Using a calendar, year planner or Gantt chart, the breeding programme should be mapped out, showing estimated dates of matings, births, weanings, disposal of surplus animals etc. The timetable should also show a cash and cost flow forecast.

Housing
You will need to have sufficient suitable cages for the initial breeding stock, plus cages for the progeny of the matings throughout the project. You will also have to ensure that you have a suitable building, or even buildings, in which the ferrets' cages can be kept. The building(s) will need to be insulated, heated/cooled, lit, supplied with electricity, water, gas etc., and be easily accessible for you and your helpers, including the use of wheelbarrows to enable the removal of waste materials. Not all ferrets will get on together, and where those ferrets are housed together, even for a short time, one or more animals may be physically damaged and injured, sometimes seriously.

Materials
Ensure that you have a reliable source for all materials you will need throughout the project. These materials will include feed, equip-

ment, cages, light bulbs/tubes, heating elements, water bottles, bedding, building materials and other such items.

Surplus Stock

Although you will want to keep some of the progeny of your breeding programme, it is obvious that you will produce more animals than you can keep, no matter how much of a ferret enthusiast you are. Plan how you will dispose of this surplus *before* they arrive; waiting until one has dozens of fourteen-week-old kits before giving thought to their disposal is foolish, and can easily become a serious welfare issue.

The Importance of Record Keeping

For any breeding programme to succeed, careful, accurate and up-to-date records must be kept of all occurrences – matings, births,

A personal digital appliance (PDA) can be used to record data, which is then uploaded to a PC.

deaths, illnesses *et al.* Whether you choose to use computers or old-fashioned paper is your choice, but whichever method you use, record everything that happens in the programme, from beginning to end; this practice will help you to spot where problems occur, and avoid the recurrence of such problems.

I cannot overemphasise how important it is to keep good records of your breeding programme. Without such records, you will not be able to repeat your successes nor avoid remaking your mistakes. I use a PC to store all records, using databases, word processing and Gantt chart software. In conjunction with the PC, I use a PDA (personal digital appliance or hand-held/palm-top computer); this enables me to input events as they happen, and then upload them to the PC when it is convenient, without information being lost, corrupted or forgotten. Never rely on your memory, no matter how good you may feel it is; memory has a nasty habit of playing tricks, whereas properly made records do not.

I am often asked what information should be recorded; the simple answer is everything that happens. The idea of record keeping is to help you to be more successful. If you neglect to record even one occurrence, that one could be the answer to many problems that will manifest themselves at a later date. I feel it is best to have too much information than not enough.

Day Book
I record every day-to-day occurrence in a 'day book'. It includes, among other items, the following:

- Matings
- Litters born
- Deaths
- Acquisitions
- Sales
- Purchases
- Bedding used
- Substrate used
- Feed used
- Visitors
- Disinfectants used
- Illnesses
- Medication administered

- Buildings and/or cages painted/treated
- Electrical failures
- Cleaning
- Veterinary treatment

There are certain tenets to which every ferret breeder should adhere. All information should be recorded as it happens, and not put to one side until a 'rainy day'. All data must be accurate, factual and complete, and records must be kept up-to-date.

Acquisitions and Disposals Record

Here at the National Ferret School, we keep an 'Acquisitions and Disposals' book. This is a large (A3), hard-backed book, with a bright red cover. The size and colour of the book helps ensure that it can always be found easily and quickly, giving no excuses for tardy and ineffectual record keeping.

As we 'acquire' an animal, it is given a number; the first animal we acquired was 00001, the second 00002, the third 00003, and so on. Every acquisition is given the next sequential number, regardless of species (as well as ferrets, we keep a large collection of raptors – birds of prey and owls – and many other types of animal). In order to aid computerisation of data (i.e. the building of computer-based databases) we use only a numeric sequence and never use alphabetical or other non-numeric characters.

It is important that *every* animal acquired and disposed of is recorded in this book. Acquisitions include animals bred here, as well as those purchased or on loan from other institutions or persons. Disposals include deaths, sales and loans, i.e. any animal that leaves us for whatever reason. Although many would question the efficiency of duplication, we now also record all acquisitions and disposals on a computer-based database. Such a database helps us to quickly and easily locate any specified animal, and all of its relatives.

In these records, we record the following data:

- Source and provenance
- Cost (if applicable)
- Date of birth or age
- Parentage
- Gender
- Colour and markings i.e. variety (if applicable)

105

- Disposition, i.e. details of other institutions/persons to whom we have sent animals
- Identification details, e.g. microchip, tattoo etc.
- Rearing techniques used, e.g. hand-reared etc.

Individual Animal Records

Every animal also has its own individual record, detailing all aspects of its life while it is in our care. This includes the following data:

- Name and reference number
- Identification marks e.g. chip number, tattoo etc.
- Variety
- Breeder, if applicable
- Date of birth
- Date acquired
- Date of disposal

These four-week-old kits are easily sexed (jill on left, hob on right of picture).

- Reason for disposal
- Parents, grandparents and great grandparents
- Siblings
- Breeding/mating details (including sizes of litters)
- Details of all prophylactics given
- Medical and health history

We have recently begun to file a digital image of every ferret mask, and of the whole animal, with a measuring device in the image, e.g. a 300 mm rule. This enables us to keep a record of the varieties and also the overall dimensions of the animal. Modern digital photography has made this task extremely simple, and also very effective.

Attached to every cage, we have a card for every ferret kept in it. These cards, once completed with the details of the animal, are laminated, and then held in place on the cage by a sturdy clip. This enables us to see at a glance every relevant detail about the cage's inmates. All writing on these cards should be in indelible

Some breeders still use books and record cards to store breeding records of ferrets in their care.

(water-proof) pen, since other inks may run or fade, despite being laminated.

These cards contain only the minimum information needed, viz:

- Name and reference number
- Variety
- Date of birth
- Identification marks etc.

The Stud Book

Many breeders use a loose-leaf folder for their stud book, and are quite happy with this arrangement. However, when using such books, it is very easy for a page to be lost, either through it falling out or simply because you forgot to replace it after removing it to copy the information. A hard-backed notebook of A4 size is ideal, and you will have no trouble with pages going missing. We find it best to either enter the details of the females at one end of the book, and those of the males at the other end, or to use two separate books. We have also computerised this stud book, using a database that allows us to produce – at the touch of a key – 'pedigrees' of any specific animal or animals. A typical page of a paper stud book may be set out as follows:

```
NAME                             REFERENCE
VARIETY
IDENTIFICATION
DATE OF BIRTH
BREEDER
PARENTS
PATERNAL G. PARENTS              MATERNAL G. PARENTS
PATERNAL G .G. PARENTS           MATERNAL G .G. PARENTS
SIBLINGS
NOTES


MATING AND BREEDING RECORD

(i.e. dates, partners, results, destination of offspring etc.)
```

Ethical Considerations

All actions regarding animals should be governed by morals and ethics; if this is not the case, we leave ourselves open to justified criticism, and this may result in the limitation or even curtailment of our activities. As stated earlier, I believe that it would be unethical to conduct a breeding programme without the intention to improve the ferrets in one's care. I also believe that it would be unethical if breeders did not keep their animals in the best manner possible throughout the animals' lives and seek veterinary treatment for any animals that fall ill. Every breeder should try to maintain the highest possible standards of health, cleanliness and care within their ferret kennels. If it becomes necessary to euthanase any ferret,

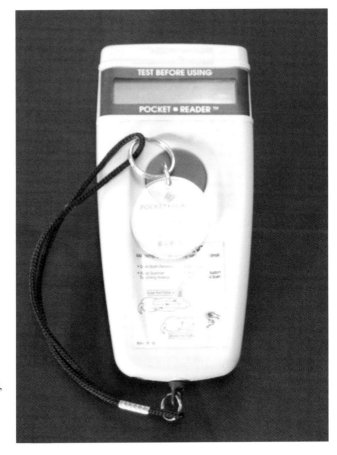

The use of microchips, implanted subcutaneously, is a proven method of identifying ferrets.

then this must be carried out in a humane and legal manner; in some areas it is unlawful for a lay person to euthanase any animal, while in others is it permitted in certain circumstances, and in certain manners. All efforts must be taken to reduce the incidence of inherited diseases, and ferrets should only be sold to those people who can give the animals a good life.

I have put together a 'Code of Ethical Practice', which can be found in the Appendices of this book. I hope readers will take on-board the contents of this Code.

Identifying Individual Ferrets

For accurate records and properly organised breeding, it is necessary to ensure that each individual ferret can be easily identified. There are several methods for this purpose, but I prefer to use 'chipping', i.e. having a small microchip inserted under the skin of every ferret. The chip should be inserted over the ribs, rather than in the neck region as, unlike dogs and cats, ferrets have little or no spare skin in the neck region. Every chip is given a unique alpha-numeric code, which should be recorded in the breeding database. Kits that are to be kept in the breeding programme should be chipped at weaning, and all of their details recorded in the database. Obviously, to use this method one must have available – at all times – a suitable scanner or reader; without one, the unique identification number of the chip cannot be read.

The First Steps

Once the brain storming has been completed, and the required animals, cages and other equipment have been put into place, one should carefully plan a timetable for implementation of the breeding programme. This timetable should be based on the following criteria:

- The ferret's physiology e.g. date of breeding condition, length of pregnancy, age of weaning kits etc.
- Date new animals required (this may not be in your control, as the animals may be required for a particular event, season etc.)
- Photoperiod; this can be manipulated
- Ambient temperature; this, too, can be manipulated

Once the timetable outline has been established, one can then fill in the details, and produce a list of jobs, and the dates on which these must be commenced and completed. I find Gantt charts extremely useful for this procedure.

All animals should be given regular 'health checks', and their condition – breeding and general – noted; all such information should be noted in the programme's day book, and also on the individual ferret's record. Most breeders find it helpful to use cards of different colours, attached to the ferrets' cages, which can indicate at a glance the relevant information. For example, one may use red cards to signify that a jill needs to be mated when she is in season, yellow cards to indicate that a jill has a litter, blue cards to show that a hob's testes have fully descended and that he can be used for breeding. Rather than cards, I prefer to use metal clips of different colours; these can be placed on the record card of an individual ferret, while the card occupies its normal position, i.e. on the front of the ferret's cage. The use of such clips prevents a proliferation of different cards on a cage, while still indicating the necessary information.

Breeding Methods

Using the relevant records of the animals in the breeding nucleus, one should establish whether to employ inbreeding or line breeding. While some – hopefully a minority – breeders use inbreeding as the norm, most do not, preferring to opt for a moderate amount of inbreeding only. Close inbreeding is defined as the mating of siblings (i.e. brother to sister) and/or offspring to parent. In the latter, it is normal to mate offspring with the younger parent, i.e. son to mother, then the daughter resulting from this mating to her father, and so on. In other, more dilute or moderate forms of inbreeding, a breeder may use one male to a few females; obviously, in this case, the progeny have the same father, but different mothers, providing that the stud male has not been selected from the same litter as any of the females used in the breeding programme. An even more dilute form of inbreeding may see several males and several females (all of whom are unrelated) used to produce litters, the pairings being on an entirely random basis, but always avoiding sibling matings, or at least only allowing them infrequently.

It is not recommended that the close forms of inbreeding are used, unless for a definite reason, and even then, only over a small number of generations. If close inbreeding is followed over many generations, then severe problems are highly likely to occur. These problems may include loss of fertility, loss of vigour, and smaller litters consisting of small, weak and 'runty' animals. With inbreeding there is no middle ground; the breeding programme will either prove to be excellent or totally unacceptable. Using close inbreeding can accurately be termed as putting all of one's eggs in one basket.

Most successful breeding programmes are based on a system of moderate inbreeding, linked to outcrosses with carefully selected animals. These outcrosses are only used where the breeder is entirely confident that such animals are superior to the ones within the breeding programme. Outcrosses should never be used simply to introduce 'fresh blood' or – even worse – simply to see what will happen if the new animal is used. Outcrosses should be used carefully, and at least initially, only on a limited basis. If all goes well, then more use can be made of the outcross but, if problems occur, then the outcross' use must be curtailed immediately, and the resultant offspring of any matings from this animal must be dealt with ruthlessly if the integrity of the breeding programme is to be maintained. A good breeder will never be afraid of cutting his losses and starting again.

A form of moderate inbreeding favoured by some breeders is line breeding. In this method, it is usual to pay careful attention to the males within the breeding programme, and not so much attention to the females; this is done for purely practical reasons, as one is more likely to use the services of a male far more than the services of a female. A male can sire a litter every few days, whereas a female can only produce one litter every few months. However, one should note that, in every breeding programme, both the male and the female contribute equally to the quality of the offspring produced. Therefore, to follow such a regime rigidly is fraught with danger. The main reason some breeders go down this route is that top quality males are more easily available than top quality females. Very few breeders will dispose of a top quality female, unless they are really pushed (too few cages, too little space etc.), whereas breeders tend not to keep as many males, and so more males with outstanding features are likely to appear on the market than are females of similar quality.

I believe it would be true to say that most line breeding occurs where use is made of the stud services of outstanding males. It is, however, impossible to found a strain of ferrets (or any other animal) without a moderate amount of inbreeding. A strain is defined as a group of related animals, each of which bears some resemblance to each other, and capable of producing consistent offspring. Some strains will be better than others, some will continually improve, while others will deteriorate. Good strains will have a steady call on them from knowledgeable breeders to provide breeding stock for their breeding programmes; these new breeding programmes may result in better or worse sub-strains, or be used by

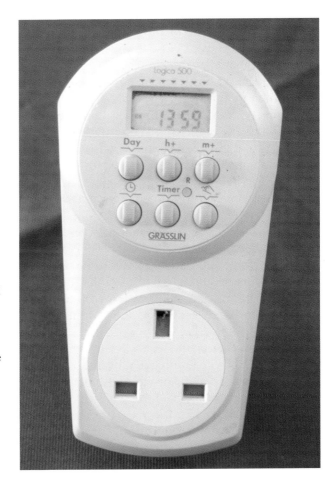

A simple method of manipulating the photoperiod of a breeding colony of ferrets. This type of time switch has an internal rechargeable battery, ensuring that the time keeping is not affected by power cuts.

the breeders to improve their own stock. The poor strains will fade away, or be improved by using the stud services of one or more top quality animals. To maintain the quality of a strain, constant attention must be paid to the state of the animals within that strain, and the progeny produced through matings. New stud animals will be needed throughout the life of any successful strain, if the quality is to be maintained.

If a breeding programme consists of only a small number of individual animals, then it will be extremely difficult to avoid inbreeding. A potential problem occurs when breeders tend to over use the services of a small number of stud males. If this happens, after a few generations, most or all of the resultant offspring will be related; even the outstanding sires themselves could become related. This need not be a major problem, providing that breeders work to ensure that they avoid close inbreeding, the number of individuals within the breeding programme does not become too small, and the top studs remain healthy.

In order to minimise the risk of inbreeding, some breeders, particularly commercial breeders of rabbits and other similar farmed animals, use a circular or rotational method of breeding. In these cases, the breeders form all of the females within their programme into direct lines of descent (usually A, B, C, D, E etc). Males from line A are then only mated with females from line B, males from line B only mated with females from line C, males from line C only mated with females from line D, and so on. Males from the last line in the series are mated with the females from line A. This procedure is repeated for every generation, and so avoids close inbreeding, and maintains the vigour of the animals. The numbers of generations required to complete the rotation of males is entirely dependent upon the number of female lines. The larger the number of female lines, the less the degree of inbreeding.

Inbreeding Depression
Where a high level of inbreeding occurs, there will be a corresponding depression of vigour or yield within a breeding programme; this is known as inbreeding depression. The increased levels of homozygosity within the breeding programme is the underlying factor that causes inbreeding depression. Inbreeding depression is sometimes referred to as the average reduction in fitness, or of a character, due to inbreeding.

If the reader adheres to the advice given earlier in this chapter, and avoids a high degree of inbreeding within the breeding programme, then inbreeding depression will not be a problem. However, where litters start to dwindle in size, the kits are smaller and weaker than normal, and adult ferrets become infertile at a younger age than would be expected (or at least have difficulty in producing litters), then inbreeding depression may be the problem. In such cases, consult the breeding records to check the level of inbreeding, and make plans to avoid inbreeding in future matings. You may even have to consider introducing an outcross, or even re-populating the whole breeding programme. If high levels of inbreeding are avoided, then such problems will not occur.

Preparing the Breeding Stock

Once the animals to form the breeding nucleus have been sourced, are safely and securely housed, and your timetable finalised, the animals must be prepared for their duties; this should have been allowed for in your planning. Both males and females will need to be kept in an area where the photoperiod is conducive to the animals being in breeding season at the planned time. If you are introducing animals into a different photoperiod, up to eight weeks may be required to allow them to acclimatise themselves to the new regime, and to allow the ferrets' body clocks to trigger the arrival of the breeding season. During this time, all of the animals should be fed a top quality diet, lower in fat and carbohydrates than normal, but higher in vitamin E. The jills, in addition, will require extra calcium and vitamin D; the calcium is necessary for the jills to be able to produce the skeleton of the kits, and the milk to feed them. Without vitamin D, the animal cannot assimilate calcium. The ambient temperature will need to be in the region of 20–25°C, in order that the hob's testes will fully descend, and he will come into breeding condition. More about the 'mechanics' of breeding can be found in Chapter 8.

At this stage, all hobs should be housed individually, as the onset of breeding condition coincides with the animal's production of large quantities of androgens, the male sex hormones. One of these androgens, testosterone, as well as bringing the animal into breeding season, will also make him more aggressive towards other ferrets, particularly other hobs. If hobs are housed together at such time, fights are inevitable; many of these fights will result in injuries or even death to one or more participants. Where hobs are housed with jills at this time, the hobs will attempt to mate the jills. As the jills will not be in breeding condition, these attempts could injure the jill(s) and/or lead to fights, where injury is almost guaranteed.

Jills housed communally may also have problems; as the female hormone, oestrogen, kicks in, jills become rather restless, and will exhibit mothering actions. These will include grabbing by the neck any other ferret within reach; these ferrets will then be dragged around the cage, regardless of their own wishes. Obviously, not all ferrets will accept this, and even those who do initially, will soon tire of such unwanted attentions. Fights in such cases are quite common, and injuries may result to one or both parties involved in the fight.

We find it best to house all hobs individually from before the onset of the breeding season. We leave the jills in their communal cages until they come into oestrus, at which time we place them with the male selected for them, whether this be a hob or a hoblet. The jills are then left in the male's quarters for twenty-four hours, and then removed to a cub of their own until the next day, when they are returned for another mating with the same hob. After this second mating, the jills are taken to their own cage, where they will remain until their litter has reached eight weeks of age. We then move mum to a cub of her own, to allow her to rest and recuperate, rebuild her strength, and receive TLC and extra rations to help her. The kits are sorted, and those selected for keeping are chipped and housed in a communal court with other kits. All decisions on the housing and disposal of stock must be fully considered before the breeding programme gets underway.

CHAPTER EIGHT

BREEDING

Checklist

Before embarking on the breeding programme, I draw up a check-list of jobs and tasks, along with dates and deadlines, as described earlier. I find the best way to plan the checklist is to use mind-mapping, and the best way to plan timetables is to use Gantt charts or PERT charts. A sample mind-map is produced on page 100. A Gantt chart is a horizontal bar chart that was developed in 1917 as a production control tool by Henry L. Gantt, an American engineer and social scientist. Frequently used in project management, the Gantt chart provides a graphical illustration of a schedule that helps to plan, co-ordinate and track specific tasks in a project. Gantt charts may be simple versions created on graph paper or more complex automated versions created using project management applications such as Microsoft Excel.

A Gantt chart is constructed with a horizontal axis representing the total time span of the project, broken down into increments (for example, days, weeks, or months), and a vertical axis representing the tasks that make up the project. Horizontal bars of varying lengths represent the sequences, timing and time span for each task. The bar spans may overlap, as, for example, you conduct research and choose your breeding stock during the same time span. As the project progresses, secondary bars, arrowheads, or darkened bars may be added to indicate completed tasks, or the portions of tasks that have been completed. A vertical line is used to represent the report date. Although Gantt charts can give a clear illustration of the project's status, one problem with them is that they don't indicate task dependencies, i.e. they cannot indicate how one task falling behind schedule affects other tasks. The PERT chart, another popular project management charting method, is designed to do this. Automated Gantt charts can store more information about tasks than can paper Gantt charts. They also offer the benefit of being easy to change, which is always helpful. Charts may be adjusted frequently to reflect the actual status of project tasks as and when they diverge from the original plan, as they often seem to.

The PERT chart is a project management tool used to schedule, organise, and co-ordinate tasks within a project, and the name is derived from Programme Evaluation Review Technique. This was a methodology developed by the US Navy in the 1950s to manage their Polaris submarine missile programme. A similar methodology, the Critical Path Method (CPM), which was developed for project management in the private sector at about the same time, has become synonymous with PERT, so that the technique is known by any variation on the names PERT, CPM, or PERT/CPM.

A PERT chart presents a graphic illustration of a project as a network diagram consisting of numbered nodes (either circles or rectangles) representing events or milestones in the project linked by labelled vectors (directional lines) depicting tasks in the same project. The direction of the arrows on the lines indicates the sequence of tasks. Where tasks must be completed in sequence, they are known as dependent or serial tasks; tasks that are not dependent on the completion of one to start the other, and that can therefore be undertaken simultaneously, are known as parallel or concurrent tasks. Tasks that must be completed in sequence but that don't require resources or completion time are considered to have event dependency. These are represented by dotted lines with arrows and are called dummy activities. Numbers on the opposite sides of the vectors indicate the time allotted for the task.

Some practitioners prefer the PERT chart to the Gantt chart, because it clearly illustrates task dependencies. However, the PERT chart can be much more difficult to produce and interpret, especially with complex projects. In industry, project managers often use both techniques. A simple alternative to both PERT and Gantt charts is the flow chart; flow chart software for PCs is readily, and cheaply, available.

Record Keeping

Start your record keeping as soon as you acquire your ferrets, and keep the records up-to-date, or they will be of little or no use. If you decide to use paper records (books, index cards etc.) in the first instance, you may still see the benefit, at a later stage, of converting to a computerised method of record keeping, i.e. computerised databases. Providing that you have kept proper, accurate and comprehensive records, apart from the work involved in keying-in all of the data, the task should be neither difficult nor onerous. However, I would urge readers to consider using computer databases from the beginning of the project; this will save much time and trouble, and allow manipulation of data (e.g. production of family trees and pedigrees) in an easier manner than if using paper data.

Housing

The alternatives for housing ferrets have been discussed elsewhere in this book, but the reader should remember that the housing must be compatible with the aims of the breeding programme, and the needs and welfare of the ferrets. It is always better to have too many cages, than insufficient numbers. The housing must be of suitable size, and the materials from which it is made must be durable and be capable of withstanding thorough cleaning.

Compatibility
Not all ferrets will get on together, and where those ferrets are housed together, even for a short time, one or more animals may be physically damaged and injured, sometimes seriously.

Hybrids and Hybrid Vigour

In the UK, many ferret owners believe that they can improve their breeding programme, and hence the kits produced, by utilising the services of a true polecat, an action fraught with potential dangers. The European polecat (*Mustela putorius*), is believed by most authorities to be the wild ancestor of the ferret, and it is believed that this species has been selectively bred for hundreds of years to produce the animal we now know as the ferret. Over those many years, breeders have selected to keep the traits that we find attractive, such as tractability (tameness), working ability etc., and discard (or breed out) the traits that we find unacceptable – biting, resenting the human presence etc. By outcrossing to a 'wild' or true polecat, breeders are in danger or attempting to re-invent the wheel. Hybrids of true polecats and ferrets will obviously be likely to carry as many 'bad' traits as 'good' traits. The most obvious result of such a cross is that the offspring, if allowed to be reared by the jill, are virtually unhandleable. Even if one raises the kits by hand, the resultant animals, although less inclined to bite than parent-reared polecat/ferret hybrids, are extremely skittish, and often resent being held for more than a few seconds.

I have a line of true polecats. These animals came originally from UK zoos, where the records indicate that the population has never been allowed to hybridise with the domestic ferret. I still breed a true line of these animals but, many years ago, I decided to try an 'experiment'. I had read many accounts of ferret keepers, who kept ferrets for working (i.e. used them for hunting rabbits – an extremely popular usage for ferrets in the UK, and one to which I am extremely fond), obtaining wild polecats and crossing them with their domestic ferrets. Every one of these authors, without exception, claimed that the animals resulting from such hybridisation were far superior at rabbiting than 'normal' ferrets. I had also spoken with many breeders who gave me

A pure polecat hob, belonging to the author.

similar assurances. I was sceptical, but decided that the only way I would ever know for sure, was to try the hybrids myself. I visited many breeders, who claimed they had true polecats, and was always disappointed when I saw these animals. Polecats are renowned for their ferocity and dark pelage, and none of the animals shown to me were dark enough, nor fierce enough. One breeder showed me his 'polecat' hob, and I was amazed to see it was an albino. The owner assured me that this was a true polecat, but that it was a mutant colour variation. When he lifted it from the cage, the ferret was certainly not very handleable, and tried several times to bite the hand of its owner, who was obviously used to such actions, and was wearing a pair of thick leather gloves. The owner told me that the way the animal was constantly trying to bite his hand was definite proof that it was a polecat and not a ferret – despite its albino colouration.

Another breeder showed me a large, fairly pale polecat-coloured hob, claiming that it was a true polecat. She lived in mid-Wales, and claimed to have caught the animal in a mink trap near to her home. She told me that the area was well known as one of the strongholds of the polecat in the UK (and it is), and that, as the animal was wild-caught, it was obviously a polecat and not a ferret. The lady then proceeded to lift the animal out of its cage (she was not wearing any gloves), and roll the animal on the floor, tickling its stomach. The animal showed no stress at this, merely a happy acceptance.

Yet another breeder wrote to me, informing me that he had caught two wild polecats in his back garden – a hob and a jill. These animals had been seen in the neighbourhood by many people, and there were rumours that at least one of these animals had been seen trying to get at pet rabbits in the area. The man had set several live catch traps, and his efforts were rewarded by the capture, on two successive nights, of the two animals he now had in his possession, and that he steadfastly claimed were true wild polecats. When I tried to point out that, as the man lived in a very urban, built-up housing estate in the centre of Portsmouth, Hampshire (England), and polecats were only believed to be living in Wales, Scotland, the Lake District and central England, he dismissed my doubts as being based on envy.

I believe that, in every case I have seen, and in most other cases of breeders claiming to have 'true wild polecats', the animals concerned are, at best, feral ferrets, i.e. domesticated ferrets that have been released (accidentally or otherwise) into the wild. It is well known that such animals can – and do – adapt to life in the wild, and in some cases will establish feral colonies, as they have in New Zealand.

Where the provenance of these 'polecats' is as dubious as the examples I have quoted, then very little credence may be attached to any accounts on the hybridisation of ferrets and polecats emanating from these breeders. It was at that point that I approached friends and former colleagues within the UK's zoos for assistance in obtaining true polecats, whose provenance was above doubt. I succeeded, and became the proud owner of a trio of un-related animals, consisting of one hob and two jills or 1.2.0 animals.

The last phrase may need some explanation. It is common prac-tice in zoos worldwide to record the number of animals in the format – males.females.undetermined (gender). Thus, if a popu-lation consisted of two males, three females and four animals which had not yet been sexed, this would be written as 2.3.4. It is im-portant to remember that the last section in this shorthand form does not necessarily refer to young animals, but merely to animals

Jills will care for their kits by feeding, cleaning and cuddling with them.

122

The offspring
of pure
polecats
belonging to
the author.

that have not yet had their gender verified. Therefore, if one was to
be given a cage containing twelve young ferrets or kits, but no one
had, as yet, sexed the animals, this would be written down as 0.0.12.
This is an excellent and much used method of shorthand.

With my new polecats firmly ensconced in their cages, I began the
breeding programme designed to discover whether hybridisation of
ferrets and polecats would result in better animals. In the first year,
I allowed the hob to cover (mate) one of the jills; the other jill was
mated by a hoblet, in order to reduce the health risks associated with

prolonged oestrus in jills. The jill gave birth to four kits (1.2.1), one of which disappeared at about ten days. It has to be assumed that the kit died and was eaten by the jill. The other three kits were left with the jill until they were twenty-five days old, at which time they were removed and hand-reared, using commercial kitten feed/milk. The kits developed well, and their eyes opened during their fifth week of life. Within a week of this, the animals were very mobile and were to be seen exploring their cage on a regular basis. The animals tried on a few occasions to nip/bite the human hand holding them. When these kits were mature, they no longer tried to bite fingers/hands, but were extremely skittish, running away from any noise or disturbance, and even the humans who had raised them. This skittish behaviour continued throughout the life of the animals.

The following year, the first jill was covered by a hoblet, and the original hob was mated with the other jill, which gave birth to five kits (3.2.0), and raised all five animals. One hob was removed from the litter at twenty-four days, and hand-reared. This was done to reduce the influence of other animals on the one kit, i.e. the last litter had been hand-reared, but all three kits had been kept together, and so could have had their behaviour affected by the presence of others of the same species. The hob progressed in an almost identical fashion to the kits in the other litter, but was slightly less skittish; this could be attributed to the method of its upbringing, or could simply have been an individual trait.

As such animals were clearly not suitable for pets, show or working, I tried another method.

1 The original hob was used to mate a ferret jill.
2 One of the original jills was mated with a ferret hob.
3 The less skittish hob from the hand-reared kits was mated with a ferret jill.

The jill from mating 1 gave birth to seven kits (3.4.0), the jill in mating 2 gave birth to six kits (1.5.0), and the jill in mating 3 gave birth to just three kits (1.2.0). All of the litters were parent-reared (i.e. left with the mother), but handled from ten days of age on a daily basis. At four weeks, just prior to the eyes opening, the kits were handled on at least ten occasions every day. Once again, the kits were skittish, though not particularly inclined to bite hands/fingers.

For the F3 generation, we used animals from the F2 generation,

Siblings showing how one kit may have both of its eyes open before another has one eye open.

and mated them with unrelated partners, all of which were normal ferrets, raising them as we did the F2 generation. Again, all the offspring were very skittish, but not inclined to bite.

We have continued this 'watering down' of the polecat genes for fifteen generations (i.e. we have mated the offspring from a pairing with normal ferrets); all of the kits produced continue to be far more skittish than 'normal' ferrets. From my own experience, I can see no evidence of true polecat genes making for better ferrets. On the contrary, based on my findings I would argue that such hybrid-isation results in far from satisfactory animals; the offspring are merely wayward ferrets with behavioural problems, far too skittish to make good working animals or pets.

The physical appearance of such hybrids is, I believe, the main reason for such breeding. The hybrid offspring of a mating between a *true* polecat and a ferret are impressive in their looks. The animals are extremely dark, verging on black, and the contrast between this black and the white of the mask is spectacular in the extreme. Whether the physical appearance of the resultant offspring is a good enough reason to carry out such hybridisation, at the cost of the loss of the ferret's tractability, is arguable in the extreme.

To a lesser degree, many breeders will look to introduce 'hybrid vigour' by using an outcross, i.e. an animal that is not related to those already within the breeding programme. By doing this, these breeders believe that the resultant offspring will be bigger, better and healthier than the kits produced by the animals within the current gene pool.

The closer the relationship, the higher the 'inbreeding coefficient'; this is a measure of the degree of inbreeding that an animal exhibits, relative to a randomly breeding population. As detailed elsewhere in this book, inbreeding can lead to a reduction in fertility, vigour and/or overall health and mental stability. In general, inbred animals tend to be more prone to diseases such as infections and even cancer, and are more likely to be of a nervous disposition or 'highly strung'.

Inbreeding tends to lead to an increase in homozygosity, while hybridisation or cross-breeding is its opposite and can maximise heterozygosity within a breeding programme. Hybrid vigour is the term given to describe how, when unrelated animals are mated, the offspring may appear to be more healthy, fertile, and of a more even temperament than either parent.

Hybrid vigour, also known as heterosis, is where the offspring tend to perform better than their parents. It is often over-rated and seen as a panacea for all poor breeding results; it is not. Like all forms of breeding, it has its place but the breeder must carry out all outcrosses with care, and only over a limited number of animals, until the results show categorically that the outcross is working. If the outcross is used indiscriminately, then the breeding programme is likely to see many problems.

Selective Breeding

It should be remembered that, in all breeding, we should be attempting to improve the ferret as a species; in addition, breeders may also be attempting to develop their own ferrets through selecting the trait or traits that the breeder sees as making the ferrets 'special'. These traits may be phenotypical (e.g. colour and markings), or relating to the character of the ferret (e.g. quiet (tame), a good worker, fast runner etc). Where a breeder produces ferrets specifically to enhance the chosen traits, this is referred to as selective breeding.

If, for example, a breeder wishes to produce ferrets of a polecat appearance (i.e. fitchets), and wishes to make the animals produced darker and darker in each generation, then he would select his darkest hob, and mate her to his darkest jill. From the litter produced by that mating, the breeder would select the darkest animals (presuming that at least one of the litter was darker than the parents), and mate it to another dark ferret. Eventually, the vast majority – or even all – the litters produced would be darker than the original ferrets.

Selection of Sire

Before selecting the hob to be used in any specific matings, the reader is urged to re-read the section on the types of breeding practices (e.g. line breeding, inbreeding etc.) in the previous chapter. Thought must be given to both the advantages and the disadvantages of each system; only then can an informed decision be made regarding the choice of stud males. Once that choice has been made, then the condition of the hob needs to be examined and action taken by the breeder to ensure that the hob is in first class condition before he is allowed to mate the jill(s) intended for him.

The hob needs to be in prime physical condition. He should be fit and healthy, with excellent musculature, a sleek coat, bright eyes, with no unusual discharges from his eyes, nose or any other orifice. He should be active and alert, and show great interest in his surroundings. His testes must both be descended into his scrotum, and he should be fed a diet high in proteins and vitamins, particularly vitamin E.

You must also give thought to the hob's mental health; breeding from a hob (or jill for that matter) with mental problems – bad temper, untrustworthy behaviour, skittish actions or similar undesirable traits – will result in offspring of a similar nature.

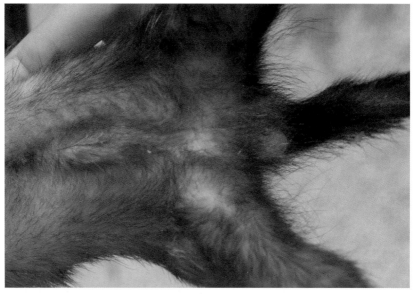

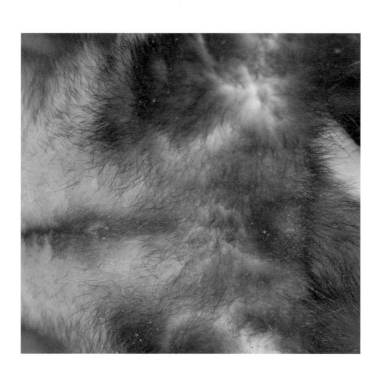

A hob in breeding condition will have both of its testes descended into its scrotum.

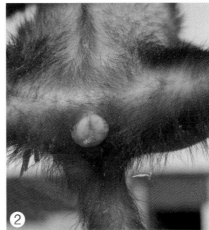
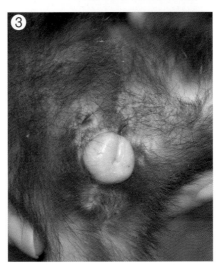

The jill's vulva will swell when she is in season; image 3 shows the jill in condition to accept a mating.

Selection of Dams

The selection of the dam requires just as much thought as does that of the hob. While some breeders believe that the male has more influence on the offspring produced than does the female, this is patently not true, as each parent gives its offspring 50 per cent of its genes.

The female should be fed on a diet high in protein, calcium and

A series of photographs showing the mating of two ferrets. Note the amount of physical force employed by the hob, and the submissiveness of the jill.

5

6

7

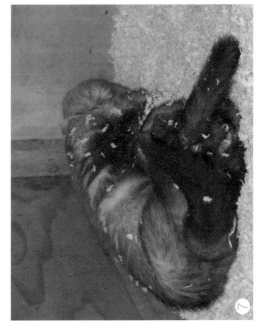

8

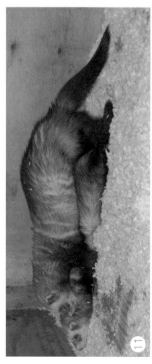

vitamins D and E; she is going to grow foetuses in her womb, which will require protein. These foetuses will have bones, which will require calcium; calcium cannot be absorbed into, and used by, the body without the presence of vitamin D. Vitamin E is the vitamin that boosts fertility.

The jill will need to be in season (in oestrus) before she can be mated. This condition is so obvious in jills that there is little need to explain too much here. When she is in oestrus, the jill's vulva (the lips around the outside of the vagina) will swell and protrude from the jill's body. The vulva may swell and protrude by up to 10 mm. At this time the vulva will be pink or even red and moist, with a slight discharge. The jill must be examined on a daily basis, in order to note the onset of vulval swelling; the mating should occur fourteen days after the vulva swells.

With both parents, it is important that their breeding history is examined, before selection is made. For instance, if the jill has been used before for breeding, and she has had difficulty kitting (giving birth), then the breeder will be able to make arrangements for such an eventuality. Also, if the jill is known to be a poor nurser, producing little milk, then necessary steps can be taken to lessen the effect that this problem may produce, such as culling the litter, removing kits to foster mothers, hand-rearing of kits etc.

As with the hob, jills used for breeding purposes must have an excellent temperament. The old stockman's saying 'put the best to the best, and then hope for the best' is worth bearing in mind at all times. Simply put, this expression means that one should only ever breed from first rate animals, but even then there is no guarantee that the mating will produce perfect animals. However, the chance of producing excellent animals from excellent stock is far greater than that of producing good animals from poor stock. If an animal with a poor disposition is mated with a similar animal, then one can guarantee that the resultant offspring will not have a good temperament.

Management of Breeding Stock

All animals within the breeding programme must be given specialised treatment, if they are to be in the required condition, and if the programme is to produce good results. Although many of these special conditions have been detailed elsewhere in this book, I feel that it would be prudent to reiterate them here.

The photoperiod for the ferrets must be given thought. Where ferrets are kept in one photoperiod and then moved to another, it will take time for the ferrets' body clocks to adjust. The optimum photoperiod for breeding ferrets is sixteen hours of light to eight hours of dark; this is known as a stimulatory photoperiod. Mature jills have a different reaction to adjustment of photoperiod from immature jills. Mature jills will come into oestrus within three weeks of being placed into a stimulatory photoperiod. Immature jills that have been kept in a non-stimulatory photoperiod (i.e. eight hours of light to sixteen hours of dark) will have their first oestrus within four weeks of being placed into a stimulatory photoperiod. This reaction can be seen in jills as young as sixteen weeks of age. Once jills are in oestrus, they will remain in oestrus indefinitely, while in a stimulatory photoperiod, or until mated or treated with hormones. Moving the jills to a non-stimulatory photoperiod will result in the jills going out of oestrus; this usually takes about fourteen days.

All ferrets within the breeding programme must be fed a high quality diet; in both sexes, high levels of vitamin E for fertility must be fed, and also large quantities of protein, necessary for body growth, repair and maintenance. The jill must be given adequate amounts of calcium and vitamin D. Calcium is used by the jill's body to produce milk during the latter stages of pregnancy and throughout the nursing period, and also to grow bones in the developing foetuses, but without vitamin D, the body cannot assimilate calcium. Therefore both are essential. In normal circumstances, ferrets exposed to the ultra-violet rays that form part of sunlight, will manufacture a sufficient amount of vitamin D (often referred to as the 'sunshine vitamin') for normal usage. However, where ferrets are kept indoors, and consequently their exposure to sunlight is low, then vitamin D supplements are needed, especially where that ferret is a jill that is to be used for breeding. A jill that has been fed inadequate amounts of calcium and vitamin D is highly likely to develop 'milk fever' (hypocalcaemia). This is caused by a lack of calcium in the blood, and can occur three to four weeks after the jill has given birth; posterior paralysis and convulsions are common symptoms. Unless treated quickly, hypocalcaemia can lead to the death of the afflicted jill and also the kits, which if they are to survive, will need to be fostered onto another jill, or hand-reared. Feeding a diet rich in vitamin D and calcium will prevent such a complication and its resultant problems.

The building in which the ferrets are housed must also have a reasonable ambient temperature; about 22°C (72° F) is recommended.

Water is essential for all life on earth. All ferrets in the breeding programme must be given constant access to a supply of fresh, clean water. Some breeders give the ferrets in their charge bowls of water, but this is not acceptable. Water bowls are too easily fouled, get knocked over, and offer the risk of drowning to young kits. Even if the kits manage to climb out of the water bowl, they may be so wet that they will succumb to a chill, and maybe even to life-threatening pneumonia. Water bottles are available from pet stores for very little cost, and come in a wide variety of sizes. For a single ferret, the minimum size recommended is ½ litre (1 pint), while for pregnant and nursing jills, a 1 litre bottle is the absolute minimum. Where the jill has a litter of over four weeks of age, then more than one large water bottle must be supplied; one drinking spout to four kits is an acceptable ratio. These water bottles will need to be

Where several ferrets are kept in one cage, a bottle may not be the best method to utilise to deliver water to the cage's inmates.

checked, cleaned and filled on a daily basis. Any spouts that leak, or bottles that have become cracked or damaged in any way, must be replaced at once.

All bottles used for watering ferrets are prone to the growth of algae; this growth can be slowed by using bottles of coloured glass; reusing empty wine bottles for the ferrets' water is a good way of doing this. Failing the use of coloured glass bottles, the bottles can be painted with black gloss, with a thin strip being left down the length of the bottle, to show the water level inside the bottle. The line can easily be achieved by using a strip of plastic insulation tape down the bottle, prior to painting. Once the paint has dried, the tape can be removed, leaving a clear strip of glass.

If several ferrets are housed together, and the breeder does not wish to have several bottles on the cage, an acceptable alternative is the drinker used for chickens. Again, these come in a variety of sizes, and care should be taken to make the correct choice. A drinker too small will not provide sufficient water, and can also be easily knocked over, while an over large drinker will be a nuisance, and will tempt the breeder to leave longer periods between cleaning and refilling. This will result in algae growth within the drinker and the consequent risk of infection/poisoning. These drinkers are made of either plastic or galvanised metal. As the galvanising process involves large amounts of zinc, a metal that is highly toxic to ferrets, these are not recommended. The plastic drinkers are ideal, but remember that they are relatively lightweight, and so very easily tipped over, unless the large size is utilised.

Where large numbers of ferrets are in the breeding programme, and/or time to fill and maintain individual water bottles is limited, then an automatic watering system is a worthwhile investment. These systems are based around a central reservoir, which is ideally connected to, and so automatically filled by, the mains water system. The central water reservoir is usually a cistern that fills via a ball-cock, but may also be a large tank that is filled by hand, using a hosepipe or even a bucket. The former is obviously much better for maintenance than the latter. From the central reservoir, pipes are run to each cage, where they terminate in nipples, from which the ferrets will drink.

While it is common and even normal for the drinking nipples on individual water bottles to be of the stainless steel ball bearing type, these nipples will allow backflow from the ferret's mouth. If this backflow were to occur in a large system, where the reservoir supplied large numbers of ferrets, it could contaminate the central reservoir, and thus every ferret being watered from that reservoir. Such nipples are not used in good automatic watering systems; instead, the nipples are designed and manufactured in such a way that they do not allow any backflow. The very best systems have nipples where the amount of water delivered through the nipple is proportional to the amount of pressure exerted by the ferret on the nipple.

Whichever system is used, it must be checked daily to ensure that it is delivering the correct amount of water to every ferret in the breeding programme. Ferrets dehydrate very quickly, and even a short time without water, especially in hot weather, can be fatal.

The Mating

When both the chosen hob and jill are seen to be in breeding condition, it is time to allow the two animals to mate. There are different ideas as to where this mating should take place, but here at the National Ferret School, we take the jill to the cage of the selected male (hob or hoblet). This cage will have been thoroughly cleaned immediately prior to the mating, and the food dish and water bottle cleaned and replenished. The jill is placed in the cage with the male, and then the couple are left together for twenty-four hours; to leave them longer is to risk injury, particularly to the jill, due to prolonged neck biting from the male. The male may be injured by the jill, fighting off his continued – and by now unwanted – attentions, though this is rare.

When the jill is placed with the male, the male will sniff at her for a few seconds. He will then grab her by the scruff of the neck, and drag her around the cage. This can go on for some minutes, until the male feels that the jill will accept him, or he has found the perfect spot within the cage to consummate their relationship. At this time, the male will hold down the jill, still biting her neck, and mount her from behind. He will begin thrusting almost at once, and may push the jill around the cage. Throughout the mating, the jill may well make shrill noises, and generally indicate that she feels uncomfortable, or is in pain; this is perfectly normal. I once heard a vet describe the mating of ferrets as akin to rape.

Once he has ejaculated, the male will continue to hold down the jill for some time, even several hours. If it is wished to produce large litters, then the couple should be allowed to mate at least twice on two consecutive days; here we remove the jill after the end of the first copulation, and return her to her own cage. About twenty-four hours after being removed from the male, the jill is returned to his cage, and another mating takes place. After this copulation is completed, the jill is taken to the cage where she will remain throughout gestation and rearing of the kits, and the hob is allowed to rest for seven days, before being used on another jill.

Injuries

Even when left for the recommended twenty-four hours, the jill may

If a jill is left too long with a hob, the jill will incur major damage to her neck.

still suffer slight injuries, and these need to be attended to, otherwise they may become infected. Initially, the cuts and bites should
be cleaned, using a mild antiseptic solution. If the injuries are fairly
severe, then it may be necessary to cut away the fur from the area.
Once cleaned, the area should have an antiseptic cream or ointment
applied. The jill should be examined daily to ascertain the condition
of the injuries. It is not normally necessary to have veterinary treatment on such injuries; providing they are clean and treated with
antiseptic, the injuries should heal well and fairly quickly. However,
if you are at all concerned about the injuries, or the jill's general
state of health, consult a veterinary surgeon, who will advise on the
necessary course of action or treatment.

The Jill's Coat

The jill's belly fur will begin to thin about two to three weeks after
mating; at full term, the belly may be almost devoid of all but a thin
coating of fur. This is normal, and is to facilitate easy location of
the jill's nipples by the kits. In addition, some jills will pull out fur
from their stomachs, and use this for lining the nest.

Pregnancy

Gestation, or pregnancy, in the ferret is a nominal forty-two days;
in reality, this may vary from forty to forty-four days. During this
time, the jill's abdomen will swell, the fur on her stomach will thin,
and her nipples will become more prominent, with the teats filling
with milk towards the end of her pregnancy.

If it is thought necessary to confirm the pregnancy, then a suitably experienced person can detect the foetuses by palpation about
fourteen days after the mating; at this stage, the foetuses will be
about the size of small walnuts. Another method that can be
utilised to determine pregnancy in a jill is ultrasonography. This is
an examination in which sound waves are bounced off tissues and
the echoes converted into a picture. The procedure is often known
as ultrasound, or simply a scan.

About three to four days after copulation, the jill's vulva will
regress (i.e. start to return to its normal size); normal size will be

achieved about two to three weeks *post coitus*. This figure, however, may be longer if the jill was left in oestrus for a long time (i.e. more than about seven days) before she was mated.

If the jill has been mated with a hoblet, or if for any other reason she has not been fertilised, then the jill will go into pseudo-pregnancy ('phantom pregnancy'). This will last for between forty and forty-two days, and the jill will return to oestrus within about two weeks of the end of this period. Obviously, the return of the jill to oestrus depends on the photoperiod under which she is maintained.

If the jill gives birth to a small number of kits, i.e. four or fewer, then she is likely to return to oestrus about two to three weeks after the birth of the litter. If the jill does come back into season, she should be mated immediately; if she is not, the raised levels of oestrogen in the jill will inhibit lactation (i.e. milk production), thus causing potential fatal problems for the kits in the litter and even the mother. Even if kept in a communal cage during pregnancy, each jill should be placed in her own cage about two to three weeks prior to the expected parturition date. If she is moved much later than this, she may well react badly. Many jills become more irritable late in their gestation, and this may lead to them turning cannibalistic with the kits.

Some breeders like to supply nest boxes, others simply give bedding, while others will do neither. We always give our pregnant jills nest boxes (one per cage), measuring approximately 230 mm wide x 240 mm high x 350 mm long (9in x 9½in x 14in); we feel that this gives the jill a feeling of privacy and security, while at the same time helping maintain the kits in the nest, in a warm environment. We build the nest boxes from marine quality plywood, approx 12 mm (½in) thick; to minimise condensation, we drill a series of holes along the top of each short side, and towards the end of one of the long sides, we cut an entrance hole about 50 mm (2in) from one end, and about 90 mm (3½in) from the floor of the nest box. The entrance hole is a smooth hole about 100 mm (4in) in diameter, and it is fitted with a closable and locking door, allowing the kits (and jill if necessary) to be confined to the nest box as and when needed, e.g. when cleaning or servicing the cage. In order to ensure that the jill's nipples and teats are not abraded, the entrance hole to the nest box must be extremely smooth and totally free from snags etc.

In the nest boxes, we lay a covering of wood shavings, and on top add soft barley straw; while some jills make quite complicated nests, others simply lie on the straw. By always supplying a quantity of bedding that exceeds the jill's requirements, she is given the opportunity to thermoregulate the nest. While some breeders use shredded paper, we never do, as we find that it becomes sodden very quickly. When in this state, it can easily form large, almost unbreakable clumps on the feet of the kits in the nest. Sawdust, a very fine material, must never be used, as it may lead to severe breathing problems for the animals in the cage.

Where pregnant jills are kept within the confines of the home, and the home owner does not wish to have shavings and straw in the house, then other methods of keeping the jill and her litter warm and safe need to be employed. A heat lamp, preferably one of the dull emitter type (i.e. one that gives out only heat and not light), can be hung about 150 mm (6 in) above one corner of the jill's cage; the nest box, which should be open-topped in this case, is placed in this corner, and supplied with a piece of terry cloth towelling. The jill

Breeding jills supplied with nest boxes feel more secure, and generally raise larger/better litters.

will use this towelling to cover herself and her litter, giving privacy, comfort, and warmth. If the cage used has a floor made from smooth plastic, fibreglass or a similar material, then the jill, and in particular the kits, will have trouble keeping their footing. This problem is easily solved by placing a piece of ribbed rubber matting (of the type used as car mats or mats to be placed on the bottom of bath tubs to prevent humans from slipping) in the bottom of the cage and nest box. If using such a mat, a second set should be available, allowing one set to be thoroughly washed each day, while the clean set is placed in the cage.

Parturition

As noted earlier in this book, pregnant jills should be housed separately; communal housing will result in the injury and/or deaths of kits and jills. In the ferret, parturition (kitting or birthing) usually occurs in the evening or night. The breeder must closely observe the jill around her due date, to watch for signs of dystocia (an inability to kit normally); signs may include restlessness, pain (usually accompanied by crying) and, if the jill has already delivered one or more kits, she may ignore those. If handled, the jill may well bite the handler, no matter how tame she is normally; this is due entirely to the fact that she is in so much pain and discomfort. It is normal for some vets to give such jills oxytocin, but this is not always the best course of action. Oxytocin induces strong contractions in the jill and, if the problem is a large kit, or a mal-positioned kit, then this may lead to the rupture of the uterus, and the separation of the placentae. The results may well be the death of the kit(s) and the jill. See Chapter 10 for more details.

Size of Kits and Litter

Normally, kits weigh 6–12 g at birth (¼–½ oz), but this weight will increase in small litters and also in litters that have gone past their due date, and kits as large as 25 g (1 oz) have been known. Obviously, larger kits such as these (in fact, any kits in excess of about 15 g/½ oz) may well cause dystocia, and must be delivered via caesarean section, if they are to live.

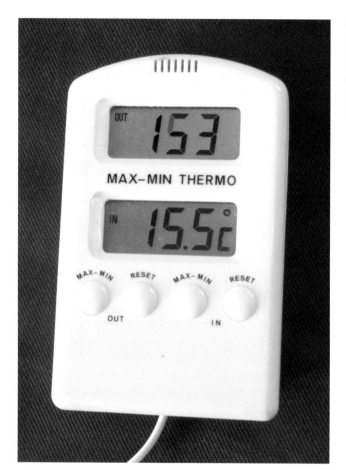

Where animals need to be kept warm, the use of an accurate digital thermometer is essential.

A normal or average litter contains about eight kits, although litters of up to twenty kits have been recorded. With large litters, supplemental feeding of the kits is usually – but not always – necessary for them all to survive to weaning. Such kits should be fed on 'milk substitute' designed for either cats or dogs. These kits will need to be fed this milk substitute six times every day, until they are weaned (at about three to four weeks). After each feed, the kits will need to have their stomachs gently massaged; this will stimulate the kits' bowels and bladder, and the massage should continue until each kit has defecated and urinated. The jill would normally carry out this function by licking the kits' stomachs and genitals.

The Animal Intensive Care Unit (AICU) is a very sophisticated piece of equipment which, although costly, is worth the investment.

To keep the kits warm between feeds, we use an Animal Intensive Care Unit (AICU) manufactured by Lyons Electrical Company. This is a very expensive and sophisticated piece of equipment that was designed, veterinary-tested and proven by Hannis L. Stoddard III, DVM. The AICU is manufactured from acrylic, which is lightweight and extremely durable. The heating console contains solid state electronics with an electrostatic filtering system, and is easily removed to allow the main plastic case to be submerged for total cleaning and disinfection. The humidity within the AICU is maintained by adjustable vents and a water tray, and the internal temperature of the unit can be maintained between ambient and 36°C (97°F). If breeding large numbers of ferrets, this piece of equipment is a good investment.

A cheaper, though less effective, alternative, is to use a heated toweling pad (similar to a miniature electric blanket), designed for use with human sports injuries. Similar pads are available for cats and dogs. All such units, for safety's sake, should be used in conjunction with a reliable thermostatic control. A temperature of about 30°C should be maintained for the kits to be comfortable. If the kits seem too hot (they will be restless), lower the temperature slightly. Conversely, if the kits appear too cold (i.e. shivering and inactive), then the temperature should be raised slightly.

Even though the jill has only six to ten nipples, she is usually quite capable of feeding up to twice that number of kits, without major problems. However, kits may have to be hand-fed or fostered when the jill is suffering from mastitis, at which time the jill will not be able to produce enough milk for her litter. Rather than hand-feed the kits, they may be placed with foster mothers; these are jills that

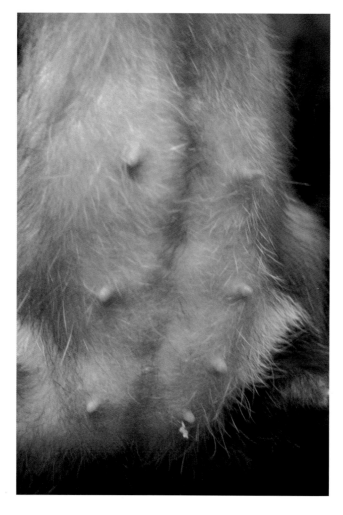

When suckling young, a jill's teats should be checked for signs of mastitis on a daily basis.

have had a smaller than average litter, and so have a surplus of milk. To do this, remove the foster mother from her own litter, placing her in a cleaned cage with some of her favourite food. Once the foster mother is in her holding cage, place the new kits in the nest with the existing kits, and gently cover the whole litter with the bedding in the nest. All the kits will then wriggle through the bedding, absorbing the smell of the jill and her original kits. The kits should be left like this for about ten to fifteen minutes, after which the jill should be returned to the cage. She will immediately start to gather together all of the kits, and the whole litter should then begin feeding from mum.

Feeding a litter will really tell on a jill and, no matter how well fed she is, she will lose weight at this time. It is vital, therefore, that the jill is allowed to feed *ad lib* on a top quality complete ferret food throughout pregnancy and until the kits are fully weaned. After the kits are removed, the jill should still be fed this diet on an *ad lib* basis for at least a further two to three weeks, in order for her to re-build her strength.

When the litter is between three to four weeks old, the jill may be afflicted by hypocalcaemia ('milk fever'– see Chapter 10 for more details); she will be particularly prone to this if she has been fed a diet low in calcium. Calcium supplementation will help avoid this potentially lethal affliction. Sprinkling dried, powdered bonemeal on the jill's food, starting about two weeks prior to mating, and continuing until the kits are weaned, is the best method of ensuring the jill has sufficient calcium to maintain her and help the kits develop a good bone structure. About 25 ml (1 teaspoon) per day is sufficient in most cases; where the litter is large (i.e. greater than eight kits) this amount should be doubled.

Frequency of Litters

The ferret is seasonally polyoestrous, normally commencing the last week of March and lasting until September, although this is dependent on the photoperiod in which the animals are kept. If the jill is exposed to a suitable photoperiod (eighteen hours light to six hours dark) throughout her pregnancy and the subsequent rearing of the litter, she will come into oestrus again about two weeks after the litter has been weaned. As mentioned earlier, jills with smaller

Even at a very early age, sexual dimorphism is apparent.

than average litters (i.e. fewer than five kits) will return to oestrus within two to three weeks of giving birth; in this case, the jill must either be re-mated or given an injection of hormones to induce ovulation, for the sake of her health. No malnourished jill should be re-bred; she needs to be given time and nutrients to allow her to rebuild her body and fitness.

If a jill is particularly 'valuable' and needs to be bred to produce large numbers of offspring, she should be maintained in a constant stimulatory photoperiod. This will enable her to have four litters in succession, with about sixteen weeks between the litters. After the fourth such litter, the jill should be rested for about six to eight weeks in a non-stimulatory photoperiod. Care must be taken with the feeding of such resting jills, since they can easily become obese if fed too much food, or are fed on a diet designed for active ferrets.

Stud hobs will need to be rested for at least one six to eight week period every year, during which time they should be placed in a non-stimulatory photoperiod, and will require a top quality diet of concentrated ferret feed. Jills have a viable breeding life of about five years, while hobs can breed until the age of eight, nine or even ten years.

Development of Kits

Ferret kits are altricial, i.e. born deaf (their ears are sealed), blind (their eyes are sealed), naked and completely dependent on their mother. Altricial literally means 'incapable of moving around on its own immediately after birth', and the word comes from a Latin root meaning 'to nourish' (a reference to the need for extensive parental care). Sometimes the term nidicolous is used to describe young that remain in the nest.

The kits' ears will open at about thirty-two to thirty-three days,

A two-hour-old kit. At this age, the kit is deaf, blind and completely dependent on its mother.

Regardless of the adult pelage, all kits at this age (two hours) are the same colour.

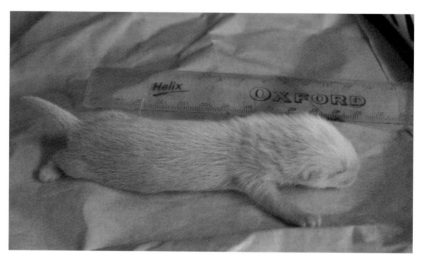

By eleven days, the kit's fur is starting to thicken.

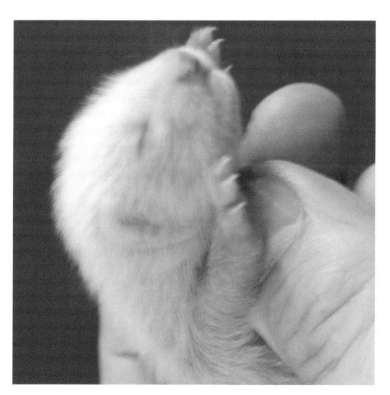

An eleven-day-old kit, showing eyes still firmly sealed.

and their eyes at between thirty to thirty-six days. The deciduous teeth will begin to erupt at about fourteen days, and will all be through by eighteen days. Between forty-seven to fifty-two days of age, the animals' permanent canine teeth will appear, and the deciduous canines will be shed at between fifty-six to seventy days. They will begin eating solid food at fourteen to twenty-one days, and should be fully weaned by forty-two days.

Kits develop and grow at a phenomenal rate, providing that the dam (mother) has an adequate supply of milk; for this, she will need a properly balanced and high quality diet. By five days of age, the kits should have doubled their size (i.e. birth weight), and their weight should be three times their birth weight by the age of ten days. It is normal for the kits' weight to increase by up to 3 g every twenty-four hours, with the average two-week-old kit weighing about 35 g. Three-week-old hob kits should weigh at least 100 g (4 oz).

It is easy to distinguish hobs from jills in very young litters, simply by glancing in the nest, as sexual dimorphism is evident from about three weeks. At this time, the hobs will be seen to be large, with broader heads than the jills; the weight of the hobs at this stage can be as much as 20 per cent higher than that of their female siblings.

By four weeks of age, kits will be venturing from their nest, even though their eyes are still closed.

Weaning

Natural weaning begins when the kits are about three weeks of age. At this stage, although the kits' eyes are still closed, the youngsters will be crawling around and exploring the nest; where nest boxes are not supplied, one or more of the kits may be found in the cage, outside of the nest. If the dam notices this, she will unceremoniously drag back the kit(s), but if she doesn't, the kit(s) may cool rapidly, leading to death. Such wanderings cannot occur where the litter is in a properly constructed nest box.

At about three weeks, the kits will start to eat the food that the jill will carry into the nest. If the breeder is feeding one of the complete diet kibbles (biscuits), then a small quantity of this feed should be wetted with warm water, and mixed with a small quantity of pork (or similar) fat. See Chapter 3 for further details.

By six weeks of age, jill kits should weigh about 200 g (7 oz), with the hobs averaging about 250 g (9 oz), and should be completely weaned. If fed on a complete diet, the average jill kit will eat about 30 g (1 oz) of food every day, and drink about 110 ml (4 fl oz) of water, although the latter is dependent on the ambient temperature.

Fading Kits

Where kits start to fade away and die during the first few weeks, this is known as 'fading kit syndrome'. There are several possible reasons:

- Congenital malformations
- Improper supplementation of the jill
- Inappropriate environmental conditions
- Inborn errors of metabolism
- Infections
- Lack of colostrum and/or milk
- Maternal neglect and/or cannibalism
- Neonatal isoerythrolysis (an immunogenic disease that affects kits within the first week of life)

Management and environmental problems may include inappropriate temperatures, poor hygiene, overcrowding, or exposure to chemical toxins. Maternal problems may include foetal retention, endometritis, pyometra or such other infections, and mastitis or agalactia. Maternal neglect of newborns and cannibalism may be associated with maternal problems and may be easily corrected by helping the jill deal with her kits; such behaviour may simply be induced by the illnesses and condition of the kits.

Kits may be stillborn or show developmental retardation and/or congenital malformations. Kits that are premature, and thus weak and unable to nurse, are likely to die of dehydration, hypothermia, or hypoglycaemia. However, many newborn kits appear healthy, active and keen to nurse, but then fade during the first few days or weeks of their life. Where the kits die suddenly, this may be caused by trauma, bleeding, congestive cardiomyopathy, sepsis, metabolic disturbances, or neonatal isoerythrolysis. Infections may be systemic or involve the respiratory tract (including ophthalmia neonatorum), gastrointestinal tract, and even the skin (including the umbilical cord). Jills may be asymptomatic carriers and shed virus under stressful circumstances (lactation, introduction of new ferrets, overcrowding etc).

Whatever the reason, fading kit syndrome should be addressed immediately it is noticed. Where the problem(s) is not readily obvious, then veterinary advice must be sought and acted upon. Delay will inevitably lead to the deaths of more kits.

The Unmated Jill

Many readers will have heard the old countrymen's tales that state that a jill must have a litter every time she is in season, or she will die. While such tales should not simply be dismissed out of hand, today we have methods at our disposal that our forefathers did not, and which can eliminate the risks of prolonged oestrus in jills, without producing unwanted litters.

If a jill is not mated when she is 'on heat', the levels of oestrogen (the female sex hormone) will build up, causing progressive depression of the bone marrow. This can result in a condition known as pancytopaenia – the abnormal depression of all three cell types of the blood. This is a condition that is potentially fatal. In other words, if a jill is left in oestrus for any length of time, she will almost inevitably die before reaching her full life expectancy. While some so-called 'experts' may dispute this, it is a scientifically proven fact,

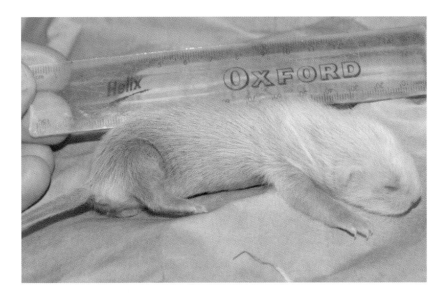

Even at just eleven days of age, a hob kit will be considerably larger and heavier than a jill kit of the same age.

and such experts should be treated with the contempt that they deserve. To leave a jill in oestrus for any length of time is cruel, and shows the owner's complete lack of care for the animal.

Where the owner of the jill does not wish to have a litter from their ferrets, the animals are best neutered (both jills and hobs); a neutered hob is known as a hobble, while a neutered jill is known as a jillette. Neutering will reduce the smell of the animals (particularly during the summer months), reduce the risk of fighting between two or more hobs, and allow any combination of ferrets to be kept together in relative safety.

However, if it is desirable to keep open all options, the best methods of removing the risk of the serious health problems linked to prolonged oestrogenic exposure are:

- To have the jill mated with a vasectomised male ferret (a hoblet)
- To have her given a 'jill jab' (a hormone injection) by a vet

To my mind, where large numbers of jills are kept, then the responsible ferret owner really cannot afford not to have at least one hoblet. The cost of having a hob vasectomised varies greatly, and so it is well worthwhile ringing vets in your area and enquiring about the cost. Once the male's *vasa deferentia* are clear of sperm (about eight to ten weeks after the operation) the hoblet will be able to take jills out of oestrus, and will be able to continue this work until he is almost ten years old, thereby repaying the investment several times over. As well as ensuring the health of the jills, savings will be made on food, time and trouble that unwanted kits would cause the owner and, of course, there will be fewer unwanted ferrets to be abandoned by unscrupulous people.

A jill mated with a hoblet will usually have a pseudo-pregnancy ('phantom pregnancy') following the mating. This may result in the jill's stomach swelling, she may produce milk and she may nest build. In other words, she will exhibit all of the symptoms of being pregnant, with one major difference – at the end of the forty-two-day 'pregnancy', she will not produce a litter. The jill will, however, come back into oestrus about three to four weeks after the end of the pseudo-pregnancy, when she will require mating again.

The physical act of mating induces the jill to ovulate (jills are known as induced ovulators). A hoblet will be quite capable of mating a jill but, as there are no sperm to fertilise the eggs, the jill will ovulate, and thus be taken out of season without becoming pregnant. Do not make the mistake of trying to use a hobble for this procedure; a hobble is a castrated male, and so will be incapable of mating the jill.

In some areas, ferret clubs recommend and encourage owners of hoblets to loan them to owners of jills in heat, but this practice is fraught with dangers; the risk of the spread of diseases such as Aleutian disease, distemper, enteritis and influenza is far too great. Encouraging the loan of hoblets simply dissuades people from making the investment for themselves, and is not a sign of responsible animal ownership.

If owners do not wish to invest in a hoblet of their own, or have only a small number of jills, the 'jill jab' – an injection with drugs such as proligestone (Delvosteron® – Intervet UK) – is often a viable alternative. It allows owners to keep their options open, without endangering their ferrets or producing unwanted litters. One of the few side effects of such hormone injections is temporary hair loss at the injection site; the hair will regrow within a couple of months. Sometimes jills will need more than one such injection during a year, i.e. if she comes back into season.

Some ferret keepers have other ideas for taking their jills out of season – some of which are extremely outlandish. One theory is that, if a suitably shaped stone or similar object is placed in the cage with a jill that is on heat, she will copulate with it, bringing herself out of season, and thus reducing any health risks. Others state that if two or more jills are kept together, and never allowed the company of a male ferret, they will 'turn lesbian' and remove each other from heat by using their paws on each other. Both ideas are, frankly, ludicrous and should not even be considered by right-thinking people.

Perhaps even more foolhardy is that some ferret owners try to simulate the coitus of a hob by gripping the jill firmly by the neck and using either a glass rod, a cotton bud or even a stick to stimulate the vagina. There is obviously a great risk of injury to the jill – and very little hope of success – in such actions, which should not be attempted by anyone.

Although a jill comes into season early in the spring (subject to a stimulatory photoperiod), and will remain so until she is removed from season by a mating or hormone injection, the obvious signs of her condition will not always be present. When she first comes into season, her vulva will swell noticeably, often protruding from her body by over a centimetre. Within seven to ten days of mating, this swelling will reduce, but it will also subside (albeit temporarily) after a couple of weeks even if she is not mated. This does not, however, mean that she is not in season as, in the next few weeks, her vulva will again swell to very large proportions.

CHAPTER NINE

REARING THE YOUNG

Care of Young Stock

Kits require special treatment if they are to prosper and grow into strong, healthy ferrets; the kits produced by a breeding programme are the breeding stock for the next season, and also the guardians of the reputation of the breeder. It makes sense to spend more time and effort on kits, if this will result in better ferrets.

Rearing
Throughout the time the kits are in the nest, the dam should be fed on a diet high in protein, calcium and vitamin D; she needs the protein and calcium to produce milk, and calcium cannot be

At twenty-one days, the kit is showing colouration of its fur.

By twenty-five days, the adult colouration of the kit is plainly visible.

absorbed into, and used by, the body without the presence of vitamin D. Her diet should also be high in calories, i.e. contain high proportions of carbohydrates and fats.

Once the kits begin to eat solid foods (at about fourteen days), you will need to provide larger quantities of food; as the kits grow, their appetite increases at a hyperbolical rate, and this is reflected in the kits' growth rate. From a birth weight of approximately 6–12 g (¼–½ oz), the kits should have doubled their size (i.e. birth weight) by five days. By ten days, the same kits should weigh in the region of 18–36 g (¾–1½ oz). It is normal for the kits' weight to increase by up to 3 g every twenty-four hours, with the average two-week-old kit weighing about 35 g (1¼ oz). Three-week-old hob kits should weigh at least 100 g (4 oz), with the jill kits weighing about 85 g (3½ oz). A weaned six–week-old jill should weigh about 200 g (7 oz); a hob of the same age will weigh about 250–275 g (9–10 oz).

Hand-rearing
It is not normal for the jill to fail to raise her litter due to lack of milk; weight for weight, the average ferret jill produces as much

milk as a good Holstein cow. Where the kits have had to be hand-reared, their weights should be approximately the same as those reared by the jill. Hand-rearing is not a task to be undertaken lightly; the procedure involves constant attention, much work and not a little heartbreak. Late/sleepless nights are also a price one has to pay for hand-rearing any animal, if one is to do it properly.

If the jill has had a prolonged and tiring kitting, she should be offered some warm food; complete diet biscuits softened with the warm juices from cooking mince is ideal. After such a meal, the jill is usually ready to begin nursing her kits. If she does not produce milk during the first twenty-four hours, then she may need a small dose of oxytocin; this should be given intra-muscularly by a veterinary surgeon. In such cases, we also give each kit a small drop of glucose solution (at body temperature) and then place the kits on the jill's nipples; almost always, the kits begin sucking, and this encourages the milk supply. For the glucose solution dissolve 60ml (4 teaspoons) of glucose per pint of water (100g in ½ litre).

If the breeder feels he must begin hand-rearing, dog or cat replacement milk is ideal for hand-rearing ferret kits, but if the breeder cannot find such items when needed, there is a mixture that is easy to prepare from standard household items. The mix is as follows:

> 1 measure evaporated milk
> 2 measures water
> 1 egg yolk per 150ml mixture (¼ pint)

The amounts in the measure will vary as to the quantity needed to feed the litter, but should simply be in the same ratio i.e. 1:2 evaporated milk to water. Never be tempted to use ordinary cow's milk, as this will cause the kits to scour, and this carries grave dangers for all young animals; neither should cow's milk be given to adult ferrets as it will have the same effect, i.e. diarrhoea. The mixture should be prepared fresh daily, and the amount required for each feed stored in separate containers, in a domestic refrigerator, once it has cooled. If any feed is left over after a meal, it must be disposed of and not returned to the refrigerator. Any feed left at the end of each day must also be disposed of. Trying to economise by saving feed for longer, will result in stomach upsets or food poisoning of the kits, and thus inevitable deaths.

The feed for each meal must be warmed immediately prior to

feeding (to about 30°C), and administered via a syringe or a kitten feeding bottle. All items used for hand-rearing must be cleaned scrupulously, and bottles, teats etc. must not be shared with different litters, to help reduce the risk of infection. A steriliser for the bottles, teats and other paraphernalia used in the hand-rearing process, is a wise investment.

All hand-reared kits will require small feeds at least six times during any twenty-four-hour period. Care must be taken to avoid over-feeding. Forcing too much milk into the kit's mouth will cause the milk to go into the kit's lungs; even small amounts are likely to lead to milk aspiration pneumonia, and the death of the kit. Too much milk being ingested will cause stomach upsets and diarrhoea, both of which could cause damage to the kit. By watching the kit's

Where kits are being hand-reared, or sick ferrets are being cared for, a steam steriliser is an ideal method of ensuring proper cleaning of feeding utensils etc.

stomach, one can easily tell when the kit has a full stomach, and feeding should stop at that point.

Where a kit has escaped from the nest, or been abandoned, it will die if left for more than a few hours. Even if the kit is found before this time, it will still require assistance if it is to survive. Such kits should be warmed by a gentle heat source until the kit is active; we then administer a small drop of warmed liquid glucose, and place the kit on one of the jill's nipples, at which time the kit usually starts sucking of its own accord.

If the litter is large, it is common for the jill to ignore all of her kits until the last kit has been born; early born kits may well chill during this time, and the jill will not attempt to nurse any cold kit. Again, the kits should be warmed and given a small amount of warmed liquid glucose before being placed in the jill's nest when parturition is complete.

Fostering

Most jills, while they are lactating, will accept more kits placed in their nest, providing that such kits are warm. To encourage kits to suckle on their new foster mum, we always administer a small amount of warmed liquid glucose to all such kits immediately prior to placing them with a foster mother. Care must be taken where kits are fostered on to a jill with a small litter; if these kits are placed with such a foster mother within twenty-four hours of the birth of the small litter, there will be no problems. However, if more kits are placed in a small litter with a potential foster mother after this time, none of the kits will receive sufficient milk, and supplemental feeding will be essential if the kits are to thrive and grow normally.

Kits that receive insufficient food will slowly starve; starving kits soon lose interest in feeding, and will quickly chill and die. Where this happens in a seemingly healthy litter, the jill should be examined for mastitis – an inflammation usually caused by an infection, leading to hard, hot, swollen teats. Such teats will not produce much – if any – milk, and the jill must receive veterinary treatment if the litter is to be fed by her. In the meantime, the breeder may well have to hand-rear the kits, until the jill has made a sufficient recovery to be able to rear the kits herself.

Agalactia, the non-production of milk, can be caused by a variety of afflictions:

- Chronic mastitis
- Mild toxaemia
- Metritis
- Pneumonia
- Too low an ambient temperature
- Insufficient or inadequate nesting materials
- Insufficient access to water
- A genetic predisposition to poor lactation
- Disturbance

Where medical problems are indicated, veterinary advice should be sought without delay.

Weaning

Many people use complicated methods of weaning the kits, stating that it is essential to provide finely chopped, or even liquidised,

Day-old chicks should not form a staple in the diet of ferrets.

food; this is totally unnecessary, and unnatural. In the wild, the jill simply catches her normal food and carries it to the nest, where she may rip off smaller pieces, but then the kits help themselves; you should emulate this behaviour if feeding meat, i.e. give smallish chunks of meat at feeding time. Varying the types of raw meat is useful in ensuring a properly balanced diet, and the addition of an occasional hard boiled egg will give you a strong, healthy litter of kits destined to grow into strong, healthy ferrets.

Where a litter is fed on a pelleted diet, this is best softened, and extra fat added. We use fat dissolved in warm water or, even better, cooked high fat content minced meat (and the water in which it is cooked) is mixed with the dry feed before it is fed to the litter. The jill will also appreciate this feed, and it will help her maintain her condition, and produce sufficient milk for the litter. The removal of all uneaten food before it has a chance to begin to deteriorate is essential, whatever feed one gives to the litter.

Where the kits have received sufficient milk, and been given access to solid food from about two weeks of age, then they should be fully weaned at about six weeks. At this stage, we separate them from their dam, and place them in a large cage with other kits, where they can socialise. The jill, which by now is almost always thin and tired, is placed into a cub of her own, and fed a top quality diet, to aid her recovery. The kits must be fed on a top quality diet, as described earlier in this book.

It is worth noting that kits will develop feeding tastes and preferences at an early age; in other words, they will develop a liking for the foods eaten while young, and these tastes will stay with them throughout their life. This process is known as 'olfactory imprinting'. This is a process in which the exposure of animals to olfactory cues during specific and restricted time windows leaves a permanent memory (known as an olfactory imprint), which shapes the animal's behaviour upon encountering the olfactory cues at later times. This is the phenomenon that leads ferrets, raised solely on a diet of a complete pelleted diet, to refuse to eat meat.

Socialisation

Kits need to be reared with other kits and also to have regular human contact if they are to be handleable when grown up. We

A thirty-day-old hob kit. Note the eyes are still closed on this young hob.

A thirty-day-old kit, with its eyes just starting to open.

start to handle our kits at about twenty-eight days; their eyes open at about thirty-two days. By doing this, I believe that the ferrets firstly get used to being handled, but also used to the sound and smell of humans; it is difficult to handle ferret kits without 'talking' to them. When their eyes do open, and they see the source of the smells and sounds, then I believe that that helps them to accept handling. They also quickly get used to seeing hands descend from on high to pluck them off the floor, and soon realise that there is no danger in this.

If you are keeping the animals as household pets, then the ferrets should be introduced carefully to other members of the household soon after their eyes are open; this includes other animals kept in the home, and with which the ferret is likely to come into contact. Where terriers are kept, and they have not been 'broken' to ferrets, even greater care must be taken, as such dogs can quickly dive in and kill a young ferret. With some terriers and other dogs, it is impossible to break them to ferrets, and so the two must never be allowed to mix.

By thirty-two days, most kits will have at least one eye open.

Early Training

Where the ferret is destined to become a pet, then the animal should be 'trained' to accept such treatment from an early age. Many owners of pet ferrets take their charges for a walk; to do this the ferret must be fitted with a suitable harness and lead. Collars do not work on ferrets, owing to the almost total absence of a neck; harnesses, which fasten both around the neck and behind the forelegs, are much safer and more comfortable.

When first fitted with a harness, the young ferret will tend to be panicked and uncomfortable. To minimise this, fit only the strap around the neck, and then place the ferret on the floor and distract

Jills with litters may become aggressive towards human hands intruding into the nest.

it with play. After a few minutes, the ferret will have almost forgotten the harness; wait another five minutes, and then pick up the ferret and fasten the other strap (behind the forelegs). Once this has been done, place the ferret on the floor, and again give it a distracting play session. Within a few days of such 'training', the ferret will have accepted the harness; at this stage, the lead can be attached, and the ferret walked in the garden, allowing the lead to trail. Again, after a short while, the ferret will ignore the lead; at this time, pick up the lead and, keeping it loose, allow the ferret to walk around. Giving the young animal food while it is on the harness and lead is a good way to get the ferret to accept the items, and associate them with good times.

A jill with a thirty-three-day-old litter. Note eyes of the kits are beginning to open.

Homing/sales

The breeder will have made up his mind as to which kits he will keep within about eight weeks of the birth of the litter. The other kits must now be passed to other homes. As detailed earlier in this book, such arrangements should have been looked at long before this time, if the kits are to be rehoused without stress for them or the breeder. Advertisements placed in appropriate magazines or shop windows are an excellent way of publicising the availability of kits. When approached by potential buyers, make enquiries with them to reassure yourself that this is not an impulse purchase, and that the buyer has all the ferret's requirements in place before letting them take the kit.

Once a breeder has established a good reputation, he will have little or no difficulty in selling all kits produced by his breeding programme. However, this is not a reason to become complacent; if the quality of the kits is not maintained, or the breeder produces too many kits, then he will be left with kits he doesn't need, want or can house properly.

CHAPTER TEN

THE MAJOR
FERRET DISEASES

The ferret is an extremely healthy and hardy animal, and rarely experiences serious medical problems. However, accidents can and do happen, and illness is certainly not unknown among ferrets. Unfortunately, ferrets are still very much 'wild animals' and as such, tend to mask symptoms of illness – often until it is too late to help them. Any unusual behaviour among your ferrets should have you checking more vigilantly, and no veterinary surgeon will mind being consulted for an animal that is not at death's door.

In some countries, ferrets are so cheap that vets rarely see the species in their surgery; unfortunately, it is cheaper and easier for uncaring owners to kill the luckless ferret than to have it treated. As more people are attracted to ferrets, and more knowledge is gained about all aspects of the animal, this sad state of affairs will hopefully come to an end.

In the UK, there is a growing problem (due to bureaucracy) whereby old, but quite effective treatments that were successfully used on what were then regarded as not 'important' animals (i.e. species other than horses, cattle, dogs and cats) have been steadily withdrawn from the veterinary market. The double whammy is that virtually nothing has replaced them, largely due to the cost of licensing. Almost all treatments for infections in 'small furries', such as ferrets, are now limited to a couple of antibiotics. Legally, for example, veterinary surgeons practising in the UK should insist that an owner signs a disclaimer every time they use ivermectin injections, and this is after the veterinary surgeon has scared their clients by having to explain all the things that can potentially go wrong.

In the UK, proposals are at an advance stage to make it a

criminal offence (not a civil offence) to prescribe anything that doesn't conform to the prescribing 'cascade'. In other words, if a veterinary surgeon chose to treat ferrets with Amfipen 15 per cent (an injection of ampicillin), that vet could be prosecuted, because the drug is currently only licensed for use in dogs, cats and horses – and in this case, there is a licensed alternative available for ferrets that could be used, i.e. Baytril injection (enrofloxacin).

For all practical purposes, this makes advice on drugs in any book fraught with difficulties. Many of the good drugs that have given sterling service and proved effective for many years, have now gone. While there are still useful drugs out there, they are not necessarily licensed for ferrets, and vets will be forced to use only licensed products, even in cases where there may well be better, but unlicensed, products available.

Diseases and Ailments

The following is a list, in alphabetical order, of some of the most common diseases and ailments that may afflict ferrets. It is not intended to be a 'do-it-yourself guide to veterinary medicine', merely to help owners recognise any potentially dangerous symptoms in their ferrets. Where appropriate, I have also included information on preventative measures that should be taken to avoid these medical problems. In all cases of ill or injured ferrets, I strongly recommend that the reader seek the advice of a veterinary surgeon; do not delay this consultation, as such time lapses can often lead to the condition of a sick or injured ferret deteriorating beyond the point where anyone, even a vet, can save the animal. Time waited is time wasted.

Abscesses

Abscesses are simply wounds that have filled with pus, the bacteria *Staphylococcus* and *Streptococcus* being the usual cause of infection. They have a variety of causes, such as bites, cuts or damage to the inside of the mouth, caused by bones in the ferret's diet. In order to prevent wounds developing into abscesses, ensure that the wounds are thoroughly cleaned and disinfected. Once abscesses have developed, they will require lancing and draining, often several times, and it may be necessary for the animal to be given a course of broad-spectrum antibiotics, such as synthetic penicillins: these include ampicillin, which has now been superseded by amoxycillin, which itself has largely been superseded by potentiated amoxycillins such as Synulox. Obviously, antibiotics should only be given if prescribed by a veterinary surgeon.

Actinomycosis

An acute hard swelling of the ferret's neck, actinomycosis is probably caused by abrasions to the animal's oesophagus, usually by feeding too many day-old chicks. This allows the organism *Actinomyces spp* to invade the membranes and tissues of the animal's head and neck; *Actinomyces* may also penetrate the animal's bone, tongue, pharynx, lymph nodes and lungs. Affected ferrets will be listless, anorexic and have a fever (a temperature of up to 40.8°C is not uncommon). Refer the animal to a veterinary surgeon, who will probably administer injections of a cephalosporin antibiotic; you will then have to keep the ferret nourished on a liquid diet until full recovery.

Aleutian Disease

This disease is caused by a parvovirus and is an immune deficiency or immune-mediated disease. It takes its name from the Aleutian strain of mink in which it was first discovered, in the United States in 1956, although it is believed that there is now a specific ferret strain of this disease. Since then, cases have been recorded in Canada (1978) and New Zealand (1984). The first cases reported in the UK were in early 1990, probably via mink imported from the United States. No true connection has ever been proven between these imported mink and Aleutian disease (AD) in ferrets, but vets and the UK's DEFRA (Department for Environment, Food and Rural Affairs) officials still retain their suspicions that this is the case.

AD is described as being transmitted both vertically and horizontally, i.e. it can pass from parents to offspring, and also from unrelated ferrets to other ferrets; this latter type of transmission occurs through body fluids. These body fluids can be saliva, blood, urine, faeces and aerosol droplets from the lungs, via sneezing, coughing and even simply breathing. This aerosol transmission can occur up to a metre away from the infected animal. It is obvious that hobs (males) should not be shared in breeding programmes, as this is an almost guaranteed method of transmitting the disease; neither should hoblets (vasectomised males) be shared between kennels of ferrets. (Hoblets are used to bring the jill out of oestrus, without getting her pregnant – vital if the jill is not to succumb to many of the ailments that prolonged oestrus can cause; see 'Oestrogen-induced anaemia'.) The number of animals reported as infected with AD is tiny.

Over the last thirty years, this disease has been investigated in great detail in the United States. This research has shown that there are at least four strains of the virus that are known to affect mink – Montana, Ontario, Pullman and Utah 1. In both mink and ferrets, the severity of the illness depends almost entirely on the strain of virus. However, the genetic make-up of the infected animal may also be a factor. At the UK's Central Veterinary Laboratory, attempts have been made to isolate and culture the virus, but unfortunately without success.

In 1986, an otter in Norfolk, England, died of symptoms that were consistent with AD. It was suggested by the veterinary pathologists involved that the infection might have come from the feral mink, though this hypothesis has never been proved or disproved.

Symptoms of AD vary tremendously, and may include black tarry faeces, weight loss, aggressiveness, recurrent fevers, thyroiditis, posterior paralysis, and eventual death; in stressed animals, death may occur extremely suddenly. There is no specific treatment, but antibiotics and steroids may give temporary relief. Diagnosis of this disease in a living ferret can be confirmed by serology, the necessary blood being obtained by clipping the toenails in such a manner that, using a capillary tube, a vet can obtain blood from the animal. With dead animals, a post-mortem examination, which should always be conducted in the case of a sudden or unexplained death, or where a disease is suspected of causing the death, will be necessary to confirm the diagnosis.

Normally, an animal's body responds to a virus by producing specific antibodies; these antibodies bind to the virus and neutralise its effects. It is only when the antibodies do not prevail over the virus, that the disease progresses. In this case, there is destruction of specific areas of tissue within the body. AD is an extremely unusual type of disease, in that the affected animals produce massive amounts of immune substances as a response to the virus, and these are deposited in various internal organs (hence the terms immune deficiency or immune-mediated disease); these deposits cause the symptoms of AD. In mink, most of the affected animals die from kidney dysfunction, while in the ferret, the symptoms are much more varied, in some cases extremely mild or even non-existent. In the recorded UK cases, the most frequent symptom was varying degrees of hindquarter paralysis. In post-mortem examinations, the pathologists found significant changes in the animals' kidneys, lungs and liver. In both mink and ferret, antibodies are produced in response to the virus, but they do not neutralise it; the reason for this is not yet known. It is this failure that leads to the persistent nature of AD infection. As the AD virus causes a degree of immuno-depression, the ferret is unable to fight off other types of infection.

Because of the variety of the symptoms of AD, diagnosis by clinical signs is extremely difficult. There is a test that can be carried out on live animals, and this is conducted on a blood sample by the counter-current immuno-electrophoresis method (CIEP or CEP). From the Utah 1 strain of the AD virus, a specific antigen has been developed; this antigen cross reacts with all currently identified strains of AD and is used in the CEP test. This test positively identifies ferrets that have developed AD antibodies, and this indicates that the animals have been exposed to the AD virus, and so it may be assumed that the animals that prove positive in this test may be carrying the virus.

Owing to the elaborate and sophisticated nature of the AD virus, there is no simple effective treatment or cure. In the United States, chemotherapy and immuno-suppressive drugs have been used with some beneficial results, but these treatments should not be regarded as practical or realistic, mainly because of the cost implications of such treatment. Neither is there a suitable vaccine for AD, and it seems unlikely that one will be produced, as such a vaccine would produce the same severe immune response as the natural disease.

No ferret having suffered AD should be bred from. All ferrets that have been in contact with the affected animal should be considered as carriers, and appropriate action (e.g. isolation, neutering) should be taken to ensure that the disease is not spread.

Alopecia (Hair Loss)
Alopecia means hair loss. It is often caused by the feeding of too many raw eggs, which contain a compound that inhibits biotin.

There are also many other causes of hair loss in ferrets, including seasonal environmental changes, and it is recommended that any ferrets manifesting such symptoms be given a thorough examination by a veterinary surgeon. See also 'Mites' and 'Ringworm'.

Hair loss on the tail can occur in either sex and at any age, the condition is often referred to as 'rat-tail' or 'bottle-brush' syndrome, ranging from a very small area of the tail to the compete tail, and in most cases, the naked skin is seen to have black spots on it; these are blocked pores – blackheads. Usually, though not always, such hair loss occurs when the animal is in its moult of late summer or early autumn, and may last for up to three to four months; the condition is also often to be seen when the spring moult occurs. Not all ferrets in the same cage will be affected, and even affected ferrets are not necessarily affected every year. Veterinary tests in many affected animals have not shown any reason or causal agents, and it is believed that the condition is simply a case of excessive moult. If in doubt, consult your veterinary surgeon.

Botulism

Botulism is a killer, and probably kills more ferrets than any other disease. The disease is caused by one of the most common bacterium known to science, *Clostridium botulinum*, usually 'Type C', a natural contaminant of most wild bird cadavers. When this bacterium comes into contact with any decaying flesh (i.e. meat), it causes a deadly toxin to be formed. If this flesh is then eaten by an animal, the toxin affects its victim by attacking the nervous system, causing paralysis, at first usually in the hind legs. Eventually, this paralysis will affect the body's vital organs, and leads inevitably to the death of the affected animal. There is no cure or treatment for this, and ferrets are among the most susceptible animals to botulism.

In order to try to prevent this deadly disease, pay particular attention to the meat that you feed; defrost frozen meat and feed immediately. If there is any doubt whatsoever about the meat, boil it for at least fifteen minutes before feeding. Botulism is not contagious and sometimes only one animal of a group may succumb to the illness. If for whatever reason you believe that your ferrets have a high risk of this disease, it is possible to have an annual toxoid injection to provide some protection for your ferrets.

Bowel Disease – See 'Proliferative Bowel Disease'.

Breathing Problems

Ferrets gasping for breath are obviously showing symptoms of some form of breathing difficulty; this may be heatstroke (see 'Heatstroke, The Sweats'), fluid on the lungs, or an obstruction of some kind. Many obstructions can be removed from a ferret's mouth with a cotton bud or even a finger.

Artificial respiration, though difficult, is possible with ferrets. If a ferret has stopped breathing, rather than give mouth-to-mouth respiration, hold the ferret by its hind legs and, keeping your arms straight, swing the animal to the left and then to the right. This transfers the weight of the ferret's internal organs on and off the diaphragm, causing the lungs to fill and empty of air. Keep this up until the ferret begins breathing on its own, until help arrives, or until you believe the ferret to be beyond help.

Cancer

Cancer is a generic term for about 100 diseases, and is a malignant growth or tumour, caused by abnormal and uncontrolled cell division; it can often spread to other parts of the animal's body through the lymphatic system or the blood stream. Where the disease spreads to adjacent tissues, it is known as invasion; where it migrates to distant cells, it is called metastasis. This unregulated growth is caused by damage to DNA, which results in mutations to the genes that control cell division. One or more of these mutations, which can either be inherited or acquired, can lead to uncontrolled cell division and tumour formation. *Tumour* (from the Latin word for swelling) refers to any abnormal mass of tissue, but may be either malignant (cancerous) or benign (non-cancerous); only malignant tumours are capable of invading other tissues or metastasising.

Cancer can cause many different symptoms, depending on the site and character of the malignancy and whether or not there is metastasis. A definitive diagnosis usually requires the microscopic examination of affected tissue obtained by biopsy. Once diagnosed, cancer is usually treated by surgery, chemotherapy and/or radiation. Although most cancers can be treated and many cured, especially if treatment begins early, if left untreated, most cancers eventually cause death.

Carcinomas originate in epithelial cells (e.g. the digestive tract or glands). Haematological malignancies, such as leukaemia and lymphoma, arise from blood and bone marrow. Sarcoma arises from connective tissue, bone or muscle. Melanoma arises in melanocytes. Teratoma begins within germ cells.

Canine Distemper – See 'Distemper, Canine'.

Canker
Canker is a generic term for ulceration, and is usually used when it refers to ear problems, when it is an inflamed, scabby condition deep inside the ear. It is often caused by an infestation of mites. See 'Mites' for more information.

Cardiomyopathy
This is a cardiovascular disease that can produce symptoms of respiratory problems, owing to pulmonary congestion, and is probably the most common cardiac disorder in the ferret, particularly in ferrets aged five years or older. The cause (aetiology) of the disease is unknown, but the condition is sometimes seen as a secondary condition to viral infections, such as influenza and Aleutian disease. See also 'Congestive Cardiomyopathy'.

Over several months, affected ferrets may show any or all of the following symptoms:

- Lethargy
- Weight loss
- Anorexia
- Depression
- Intolerance of exercise
- Respiratory distress
- Cyanosis of the mucous membranes of the mouth and nose
- Hypothermia
- Hind leg weakness or paralysis

Radiography and ultrasonography are used to diagnose this condition, and will show an enlarged ball-shaped (globoid) heart. Treatment for this condition is intended to improve the function of the heart, and may include giving the affected animal oxygen and diuretics. The prognosis of cases varies, and treatment failure is fairly common.

Cataracts

A cataract is a clouding, or opaqueness of the lens of the ferret's eye; they may affect one or both eyes. When untreated, the cataract causes the ferret's vision to blur. Cataracts occur naturally in older ferrets, but exposure to too many ultraviolet rays can cause them in ferrets of almost any age. In humans, treatment is by surgical removal of the affected lens(es), and replacement with a synthetic lens. Such treatment is not available for ferrets. In most ferrets affected by cataracts, the animals seem not to notice, and the condition is certainly painless. As the ferret's eyesight is normally poor, except at close range, and the animal depends more on its other senses to obtain a picture of the world, then it is possible that the ferret may not even notice the condition. It is also unlikely to affect the ferret's behaviour.

CD or CDV – See 'Distemper, Canine'.

Congestive Cardiomyopathy

Probably the most common cardiac condition in middle-aged and older ferrets, congestive cardiomyopathy is often a secondary disease in animals suffering from viral infections. Animals affected by this condition may be lethargic, depressed, show weight loss and anorexia, be intolerant of exercise, and have problems breathing (respiratory distress) over a long period (several months). When examined, there may be cyanosis (a bluish coloration of the skin, mucous membranes, and nail-beds, resulting from a lack of oxygenated haemoglobin in the blood), hypothermia and muffled heart and lung sounds. The affected ferret may also show weakness in the hind legs. Radiography, ECG and ultrasound may be used to confirm the diagnosis. Treatment for this condition is intended to improve the function of the heart, and may include giving the affected animal oxygen and diuretics. The prognosis of cases varies, and treatment failure is fairly common.

Dehydration

Dehydration is a condition caused by the loss of too much fluid from the ferret's body. It is often caused, or exacerbated, by severe diarrhoea or vomiting. To test if a ferret is dehydrated, pinch a fold of skin on the ferret's flank, and pull it out slightly. On release, the

Within a court, where several ferrets are kept together, it is necessary to supply several feeding dishes and a large water container for the ferrets.

skin should return to normal almost instantly; if it does not, the animal is dehydrated.

While diarrhoea and vomiting can cause dehydration, it can also be caused by feeding dry feed without supplying the ferret with an adequate supply of clean drinking water, or by keeping the ferret in a warm environment and limiting its access to water. The condition of a dehydrated ferret will quickly deteriorate, resulting in death, unless the animal is rehydrated quickly. In many cases, the animal can be given rehydrating fluid to drink; such fluids are readily available at veterinary surgeries and pet shops. However, if a dehydrated ferret is found and the owner has no such fluid, an effective substitute can be made by mixing:

- ½ litre (1 pint) warm water
- 15 ml (1 tablespoon) sugar*
- 5 ml (1 teaspoon) salt

* Where it is available, glucose is better than household sugar, as it is more easily assimilated by the affected animal.

The mixture should be given to the ferret *ad lib* for about twenty-four hours. By checking the elasticity of the ferret's skin, the owner will be able to tell if it is rehydrating. When we have a ferret suffering from vomiting or diarrhoea, we always give rehydrating fluid in place of water.

In acute and severe cases of dehydration, veterinary advice should be sought. In severe cases, a vet may administer a re-hydrating solution intravenously (i.e. via the blood stream, through a hypodermic needle) or by injecting directly into the animal's abdomen (peritoneum).

Dental Problems

Ferrets, like humans, occasionally have dental problems, particularly older ferrets. They occasionally damage their teeth, either while working or even in their cage when chewing the wire mesh; gingivitis, a gum disorder, is also quite common in ferrets. The build-up of food debris often leads to dental problems, and the diet of the ferret is, therefore, an important factor in the condition of the teeth.

Where the ferret is fed a diet of soft food (e.g. tinned cat or dog food), periodontal (affecting tissue and structures surrounding and supporting the teeth) disease and dental calculus (a hard yellowish deposit on the teeth, consisting of organic secretions and food particles deposited in various salts, such as calcium carbonate, sometimes referred to as tartar) are present. The treatment for this condition usually involves the anesthetised ferret having its teeth scaled and polished.

Some ferrets develop stereotypical behaviour involving biting solid objects, such as the bars of their cage; broken teeth are fairly common with such animals. Root canal treatment or extraction of the offending tooth constitute the treatment for such afflictions. Tooth root abscesses occasionally occur in the ferret; in these cases, the tooth needs to be extracted and the ferret treated with anti-biotics. Any problems with a ferret's teeth must be treated by a veterinary surgeon.

Diarrhoea

Diarrhoea is a symptom and *not* a disease; it is indicative of a problem, which may be serious or minor, but will still require investigation. In ferrets, this condition is often referred to as 'the scours', and is often, but of course not always, a sign that the animal has been fed a poor diet, or its food is contaminated. Feeding milk sops, too many raw eggs, too much fat, a sudden and abrupt change of diet, and food that has gone off all have the effect of scouring a ferret. Diarrhoea can also be indicative of some other, more serious, affliction, such as poisoning, internal parasites or even stress.

If you are feeding your ferrets a proper balanced diet of fresh, or freshly defrosted, cadavers, they should not suffer from loose motions as a matter of course. If you have been feeding them on a diet of bread and milk, their motions will almost always be soft (often liquid), light brown in colour, and extremely smelly. If fed on the diet that I have recommended in Chapter 3, their motions will be solid, almost black, and have little smell. Keep a record of everything you feed them, particularly anything out of the ordinary.

Diarrhoea causes the animal to dehydrate, and can lead to irreparable body damage, particularly of the kidneys, and even death. The affected ferret(s) should be isolated, and kept on a water and electrolyte (rehydrating) regime (see 'Dehydration') for twenty-four hours, dosing with kaolin solution about every two hours. After the fast, food intake should be gradually built up again; do *not* put the animals straight back on their original diet, otherwise the whole problem may recur. Chicken, rabbit and fish are excellent 'invalid' foods, and ideal for this task.

If the diarrhoea persists, or if there is blood in the motions, the veterinary surgeon must be consulted immediately.

Distemper, Canine (CD)

Ferrets are highly susceptible to canine distemper, a virus that is one of the most common fatal diseases in ferrets, with almost 100 per cent mortality; dogs are the most common source of infection, with the incubation period being between seven and nine days. In some countries, owners have their animals vaccinated against this disease as a matter of course, while in others this does not happen. Indeed, in some countries there is no distemper vaccine licensed for use in ferrets; the use of an unsuitable vaccine may have fatal results. If you are considering this preventative course of action, consult your veterinary surgeon.

There are different strains of CD, some of which cause mainly respiratory symptoms, while others cause problems in nerve tissues;

such symptoms are known as neurotropic signs. CD always leads to secondary bacterial infections; these complicate the diagnosis of the condition and may well have an adverse effect on the outcome of the treatment.

Symptoms of the disease may include swollen feet (leading to hard pad, the actual thickening of the soles of the feet and a classical sign of distemper infection), runny eyes and nose, diarrhoea, lack of appetite, a greater than average thirst and a rash, usually under the chin. In its latter stages, the infected animal will vomit, have convulsions and, shortly before dying, will pass into a coma.

This disease is highly contagious and, at the first signs of distemper, all infected ferrets must be isolated. Ensure that you thoroughly disinfect your hands after handling a sick animal; as the name suggests, dogs can also contract this disease, and it is all too easy to spread it. Immediate veterinary advice must be sought, although only very mild cases can be treated; it is often kinder, both to the infected ferrets and the others in your care, to have the infected ferret put down once the diagnosis is confirmed by a veterinary surgeon. A dose of immune serum (e.g. Maxagloban P™, Hoechst) will give your ferrets a passive immunity. This drug is administered either subcutaneously (SC) or intramuscularly (IM), and will give passive immunity for two to three weeks.

The virus is spread by airborne droplets, and can survive in the environment for quite long periods. After any outbreak of CD, all cages, utensils and surfaces in the ferret kennels and cages must be thoroughly cleaned with an appropriate disinfectant. The virus is also shed in discharges and excreta from the affected ferrets, and so all soiled substrate, bedding and other waste should be burned.

In the UK, CD in dogs is relatively rare, due mainly to the vaccination process; accordingly, CD in UK ferrets is also very low. In some parts of the world, the opposite is true. Seek veterinary advice on the current availability and need for vaccinating ferrets in your area, and follow the recommended procedure on boosters etc.

Dystocia

Dystocia is a generic term for an inability to kit normally. Signs may include restlessness, pain (usually accompanied by crying) and, if the jill has already delivered one or more kits, she may ignore those. If handled, the jill may well bite the handler, no matter how tame she is normally; this is due entirely to the fact that she is in so much pain and discomfort. It is normal for some veterinary surgeons to give such jills oxytocin, but this is not always the best course of action. Oxytocin induces strong contractions and, if the problem is a large kit, or a mal-positioned kit, then this may lead to the rupture of the uterus, and the separation of the placentae. The result may well be the death of both the kit(s) and the jill.

Dystocia is sometimes caused by congenitally defective kits. These kits could well be the result of deleterious genes, such as the breeding of 'silver' or 'blue' ferrets, since this variety is known to have severe problems with congenital defects and generally poor reproduction. So-called black-eyed whites (which actually have extremely dark ruby eyes) are also known to have similar problems. In such cases, these abnormalities – which include cleft palates and cyclopia (a congenital facial abnormality) – may cause abnormal delivery of the litter, even though only a small number of the litter has the problem. In some such cases, though by no means all, the administering by a vet, of prostaglandin may help. Very often, if the jill is to be saved, a veterinary surgeon may need to carry out a caesarean section.

Endocrine Alopecia

When alopecia is seen with no scratching, rubbing, biting, or licking, the cause is usually a result of some disruption in normal hair growth. Endocrine alopecia in ferrets is a condition where the hair loss is caused by an excess or deficiency in hormones. The normal hair cycle includes phases of growth, rest, and shedding, and each of these phases is controlled by various growth factors, including hormones. If the growth part of the cycle is defective, new hairs fail to grow, and so the entire hair cycle stops. Control of the hairs varies with different parts of the body, so hair loss can sometimes be seen on one part of the ferret's body while the hairs on the rest of its body appear normal. There are many factors that affect the hair cycle, including photoperiod, nutrition, hormones and growth factors.

When a ferret has endocrine alopecia, most of the hairs on the trunk and tail are affected, sometimes leaving just a thin, silky covering, and sometimes resulting in total loss of the fur on this area. A deficiency in testosterone, thyroid hormone, or oestrogen and an excessive amount of cortisol can cause endocrine alopecia.

The pattern of hair loss caused by hormone problems is characterised by hair loss on the trunk and tail; the head and legs are often unaffected.

Diagnosis is by physical examination and blood tests, and treatment can only be achieved after the cause is determined. Replacement hormones may be prescribed, but some forms of endocrine alopecia do not respond to treatment. If left untreated this condition will eventually lead to the death of the ferret.

Enteritis

Enteritis is an inflammation of the intestines, causing diarrhoea, and is very common among kits and young stock. If your ferrets are experiencing diarrhoea, and show signs of blood in their diarrhoea, it may indicate this condition. It can be caused by different things but, usually, it is the bacterium *Escherichia coli* (often referred to by its abbreviated name of *E. coli* and formerly known to science as *Bacillus coli*). Immediate treatment with a broad spectrum antibiotic, supplemented with regular doses of kaolin, may cure this condition. If left untreated, the affected animal will most definitely die. Another major cause of enteritis is *Campylobacter spp*; in humans, this type of 'food poisoning' is known as dysentery. The most effective antibiotics for use against this are currently chloramphenicol and gentamicin. As mentioned under the heading 'diarrhoea', affected animals must be given large amounts of water and electrolyte to avoid the dangers associated with dehydration.

Foot Rot

This condition was extremely common until quite recently, and in some areas is still a major problem. It is usually caused by keeping ferrets in dirty, wet conditions, allowing a mite, *Sarcoptes scabiei*, to infect the animals. The symptoms of foot rot are swollen, scabby feet and, if left untreated, the claws will eventually drop off. Affected animals must be isolated immediately, and all other ferrets – especially those kept in the same cage – examined. All bedding and wood shavings must be removed from the cage and burned, with the cage itself being thoroughly disinfected with a suitable disinfectant. Veterinary treatment must be sought for all infected ferrets, as home treatment is only very rarely effective; time waited is time wasted.

Gall Stones – See 'Urolithiasis'.

Gastritis

This is an inflammation of the stomach, and may have several causes, including poisoning, a foreign body or internal parasites; very often there is more than one cause. Symptoms of gastritis may include lethargy, anorexia and weight loss, vomiting, tooth grinding (due to abdominal pain and nausea), dehydration, and ptyalism (an excessive flow of saliva). Where the ferret produces black, tarry scats (stools), this may indicate gastro-duodenal ulceration.

Diagnosis of this problem will include clinical examinations, and possibly radiography and examination of scats and vomit. The treatment for most cases simply involves the administration of supportive care, with small but frequent meals of bland food. Where a foreign body is the cause, it will need to be surgically removed before such care can be undertaken.

Hard Pad – See 'Distemper, Canine'.

Heatstroke (The Sweats)

Ferrets cannot tolerate high temperatures, reacting adversely to too much heat, and may well die from heat-stroke, often referred to as 'the sweats', a rather misleading term, since ferrets cannot sweat. As in all things, prevention is better than cure, and the siting of the cage (as discussed in an earlier chapter) is very important, as is the position that they are left in while out working. In the confines of a carrying box or even a motor car, the temperature can quickly rise to a dangerous level, even in the cooler sunshine of autumn and spring. No animals should be left unattended in a vehicle, or transported in such a manner that they or their carrying box is in full sunlight; the sun does not stay in the same position throughout the day, and, even if the box or car is in the shadows when you leave it, it may not stay that way for long. When you return, your ferrets may well be dead.

Hypothermia

Hypothermia is an abnormally low body temperature. The normal body temperature of a ferret is 38.6° C, with a range of 37.8 to 40°C. With significant hypothermia, a ferret becomes physically and mentally sluggish, and with severe hypothermia, it is likely to become unconscious. It is essential, once a ferret has been diagnosed as suffering from hypothermia, to start to warm the animal *slowly*. If you have access to water of varying temperatures, or a means of warming water, start by placing the ferret in cool water and gradually increase the temperature of the water over a couple of hours. If hypothermia besets a ferret while you are in the field, wrap a 'space blanket' around the animal. A small heat pack, of the type carried by sportsmen and women, can be placed close to the afflicted ferret, but should never be placed on the animal, as localised heat can cause problems. Have the ferret assessed by a veterinary surgeon as soon as possible.

Hypocalcaemia

A lack of calcium in the blood, this affliction can occur three to four weeks after the jill has given birth. Posterior paralysis and convulsions are common symptoms, while the cause is usually due to poor diet; feeding a diet heavily dependent on day-old chicks will almost certainly lead to this complaint. Consult your veterinary surgeon immediately; he will probably administer an intra-peritoneal injection of calcium borogluconate, which gives a speedy response in affected animals. After this injection, a calcium-rich diet is essential for total recovery.

Influenza

Ferrets are susceptible to the human influenza virus as well as other mammalian strains, and can catch influenza, (the flu) from their owners, or vice versa; influenza is both zoonotic and anthro-zoonotic. Symptoms in ferrets are the same as in humans – fever, sneezing, lack of appetite, listlessness, runny eyes and a nasal discharge. In adult ferrets, the condition is not usually serious, with most ferrets making a spontaneous recovery, although antibiotics may be necessary to control some secondary infections. Influenza is, however, almost always fatal in young ferrets. Infected ferrets must be isolated to prevent spread of this condition. The wearing of a mask by humans will help prevent the crossing of the infection from ferret to human, and vice versa.

Leptospirosis

The ferret has a natural resistance to this disease, often called 'rat catcher's yellows' or 'Weil's disease', and is highly unlikely to contract it. Consequently, vaccinations for leptospirosis are unnecessary and should not be used.

Leukaemia

This disease is often found in unmated jills, but is almost completely undetectable until the ferret is almost at death's door. The presence of any 'lumps' in the animal's groin or abdomen, or under the jaw, may indicate this disease. Medical advice should be sought immediately. See also 'Oestrogen-induced Anaemia'.

Mange – See 'Mites'.

Mastitis

This is an inflammation of the jill's mammary glands, and often occurs when the jill is in the early stages of feeding young. It is a very painful condition that requires immediate medical attention. The glands become very swollen and hard and the kits can obtain very little – if any – milk. Unless it is cleared up quickly, the kits will probably die and the jill will, at best, be very ill. The disease is caused by infection by *E. coli*, and treatment usually consists of antibiotics.

Mites

Mites have unpleasant effects on the ferret, and there are three types commonly found on the animal. *Sarcoptes scabiei* causes two types of mange in ferrets, which can be caught by coming into direct contact with other affected animals, such as rodents, or simply by being on contaminated ground. One type of mange causes alopecia and pruritis (an intense itching), while the other causes only foot or toe problems (foot rot). The first sign of mange is persistent scratching, even though there is no obvious cause such as fleas. Eventually, the skin will become very red and sore, a symptom that is easier to notice in albino ferrets than in ones with polecat colouration. As the disease progresses, these sores cause baldness and the sores become even worse.

A parasiticidal wash must be applied to the affected areas, or injections of a broad-spectrum anti-parasitic drug administered; drugs of this type cannot be used in the first month of pregnancy, as they could cause congenital defects. The cage must be thoroughly treated, soaking it in a strong solution of disinfectant or bleach, which must be washed off before any ferret is returned to the cage.

Be warned – mange can be contracted by humans, when it is known as scabies.

Ear mites, *Otodectes cynotis*, are common in ferrets and can cause canker. The mites can easily be treated with ear drops that contain monosulfiram or with a broad-spectrum anti-parasitic. If your ferrets seem to spend a lot of time scratching their ears, an investigation is called for. A build-up of wax in the ears, dotted with black specks, is a sure indication that ferrets have ear mites; the black specks are probably spots of dried blood. The ear mites are usually white or colourless and are just about visible to the naked eye (they are the largest mites to affect 'small animals'), a magnifying lens or an otoscope being required to clearly see these tiny animals. If left untreated, the irritation caused by these mites will cause the ferret to scratch, sometimes until its ears bleed. The mites can move down the aural canal and, if the eardrum has been ruptured, infect the middle ear; such an infection will cause the affected animal to lose its sense of balance. This may be indicated either by the ferret simply being unable to hold its head straight or, in more serious cases, by constantly falling over. It is important that all ferrets that have been in contact with the infected ferret are also treated, as ear mites can infect other animals which may not show any symptoms for some time. Seek veterinary advice in all cases of ear mite, loss of balance etc.

The harvest mite, *Trombicula autumnalis*, can cause sores on the underside of the neck and trunk of ferrets, particularly during the autumn period; a wash in a suitable insecticidal shampoo may help. Your veterinary surgeon will advise you on suitable treatments.

Oestrogen-induced Anaemia

When a jill is not mated, the levels of oestrogen (the female sex hormone) in her body rise and can have serious effects on her health. This frequently leads to progressive depression of the bone marrow, often resulting in a condition known as pancytopaenia – the abnormal depression of all three elements of blood – which is debilitating and potentially fatal. Signs include weight loss, alopecia, anorexia, pale lips and gums, difficulty in breathing and, in later stages, darkening of faeces (caused by blood), and bleeding sores on the animal's flanks and abdomen. There may also be secondary infections.

In its advanced stages, treatment is highly unlikely to be effective.

However, in the early stages, spaying or hormonal treatment to stop oestrus may be used with repeated transfusions of fresh whole blood containing 1 ml of sodium citrate.

Again, prevention is better than cure, and jills that are not wanted for breeding from should be neutered (spayed), or given drugs (e.g. proligestone), or served with a hoblet (a vasectomised male ferret). The latter course of action will almost certainly result in a 'phantom pregnancy' (pseudo-pregnancy), which will last for the full forty-two-day term, after which the jill will return to oestrus, and need to be served again.

Osteodystrophy

Defective bone formations, often due to hyperphosphorosis (too much phosphorous in the diet) are caused by feeding a diet consisting entirely of, or rich in, muscle meat; this lacks calcium, and leads to a deficiency of this vital mineral. The problem usually manifests itself in young ferrets (six to twelve weeks), which have difficulty walking, moving instead with the gait of a seal, with the legs (particularly the front legs) sticking out to the side of the body rather than pointing to the floor; death is common. As the bones of such animals are soft and deformed, the ferrets never completely recover, and will always have deformed legs and spine, making movement awkward, difficult and painful. A top quality vitamin and mineral supplement can help, but it is better to prevent the problem by feeding a diet of complete cadavers, rather than 'meat'. Veterinary advice must, of course, be sought whenever ferrets have difficulty walking in a normal manner.

Parasites –See also 'Mites'.

Even the most pampered ferrets can suffer from the unwanted attentions of parasites, either internal (endoparasites) or external (ectoparasites). Ferrets can suffer from worms, *Toxocara* or *Toxascaris*. A vet will prescribe an anthelmintic (an agent that is destructive to worms) such as mebendazole or fenbenzadole (e.g. Panacur). Panacur is available in both oral suspension and granules; we prefer the oral suspension. The dosage for Panacur is 1 ml per kilo of body weight. In the interests of all concerned, ferrets should be treated for worms every six months, and always before a jill is mated. Panacur is a relatively safe drug, although some animals may experience vomiting or nausea after deworming.

Fenbenzadole is considered safe for use in pregnancy in all species. Treatment is necessary for three consecutive days, and depending on which parasite is being treated, treatment may require a second course.

Heart worms, coccidia, *Toxoplasma*, and *Pneumocystis* are sometimes found. Veterinary examination, and clinical investigation of the faeces, will be necessary to positively identify the actual problem.

The first sign of a worm infestation is an insatiable appetite coupled with a steady loss of weight. Sometimes, if the ferret is infected by tape worms, segments of the worms may be found in the ferret's faeces; *Toxocara* and *Toxascaris* are roundworms, and *not* segmented. Do not attempt to treat ferrets with powders and doses that your local pet shop may recommend for a dog. Seek veterinary advice.

Fleas (*Ctenocephalides spp*) and ticks (*Ixodes ricinus*) are external parasites that most working ferrets will catch at some stage, especially if used for hunting; these ectoparasites are contracted from other animals such as dogs, cats and rabbits. Most insecticidal preparations intended for dogs and cats are safe to use on ferrets. With new preparations coming on to the market all the time, care must always be taken to ensure that any product is safe *before* you use it on your ferrets. Do not forget that you will have to adjust the dosage to suit the size of the ferret, as per the manufacturer's instructions.

All of the bedding and wood shavings from the ferret's cage must be removed and burned, and the cage thoroughly disinfected. Use a good insecticide as a prophylactic (preventative measure) to treat all shavings, bedding and even the cage itself; this insecticide must be suitable and harmless to the ferret – seek veterinary advice. Do not use such powders and sprays in any cage where a jill is still feeding her kits, as there is a danger of poisoning the litter.

Ticks are rather more difficult to deal with than fleas, but they do respond to some sprays and powders and spot-on preparations, although in some countries, these may only be available from veterinary surgeons. Care must be taken to ensure that the mouth parts of ticks are completely removed from the ferret's skin, otherwise infection and abscesses can occur; never simply pull ticks out. Paint alcohol on the tick using a fine paintbrush. The tick should have died and dropped off within twenty-four hours; if not, simply repeat the process. Although some authorities suggest that ticks be burned off with a lighted cigarette, this should never be attempted. It is all too easy to burn the ferret and the alcohol method is much more effective, with none of the dangers.

There are now a number of devices on the market that have been specifically designed to remove ticks, mainly produced in response to concern regarding Lyme's disease in humans. These are a type of sprung forceps that grip the tick around the head; the device is then gently twisted backwards and forwards, until the tick comes out. We have tested several such implements, and have had 100 per cent success with each; we now keep one in all of our first aid kits.

Pneumonia

When a ferret is suffering from a viral infection, such as canine distemper, Aleutian disease etc., the animal may well contract bacterial pneumonia as a secondary infection; the usual culprits for such secondary infections are bacteria such as *Escherichia coli*, *Proteus vulgaris, Klebsiella pneumoniae* and *Pseudomonas aeruginosa*. While this is the most common type of pneumonia to afflict ferrets, they may also suffer from primary pathogens, such as *Streptococcus zooepidemicus* or *Pasteurella pneumotropica*. These pathogens invade the respiratory tract, causing pneumonia. When ferrets inhale milk, medication or even vomit, this can lead to aspiration pneumonia.

The symptoms of pneumonia in ferrets may include any or all of the following:

- An increase in abdominal respiration
- Anorexia
- Cyanosis (a bluish coloration of the skin, mucous membranes and nail-beds, resulting from a lack of oxygenated haemoglobin in the blood)
- Dyspnoea (difficulty in breathing, or shortness of breath disproportionate to effort)
- Fever
- Lethargy
- Nasal discharge

If the animal is suffering from fulminant pneumonia (i.e. a pneumonia that occurs suddenly, rapidly, and with great severity or intensity), there is likely to be little or no indication of any symptoms; this type of pneumonia causes sudden death, but is rare in ferrets.

Diagnosis of this disease requires radiography, which will show an increased density in the lungs; culturing of tracheal exudates may also be used. Treatment consists of drug therapy (penicillin, potentiated sulphonamides or enrofloxacin), while oxygen and diuretics – in conjunction with force feeding – may be used to improve the animal's general condition. Depending on the cause of the infection, steps must be taken to prevent recurrence, e.g. isolating affected ferrets, care with oral administration of feed and/or medicines etc.

Posterior Paralysis (The Staggers)
The causes of paralysis in ferrets are many and varied, including disease of the spinal disks, hypocalcaemia (lack of calcium in the blood), Aleutian disease, viral myelitis (inflammation of the spinal cord), cancer of the spine, vertebral trauma, or even a dietary deficiency. It is often caused by injury, and paralysis can also be inherited. If the latter is the case, the disorder will show itself in young litters. There is usually no cure for this and it is, therefore, best to have the animals destroyed. The parents of such litters should not be used for breeding again. In all cases of paralysis, veterinary advice must be sought immediately.

Pregnancy Toxaemia
Leading to the sudden death of the jill just before she is due to give birth, the cause of this problem is currently unknown, but is probably linked to a poor diet.

Proliferative Bowel Disease
This is a disease that affects young (less than fourteen months) ferrets, particularly males. Proliferative bowel disease may begin as acute colitis (inflammation of the colon), producing greenish diarrhoea, speckled with blood. Defecation causes pain to the affected ferret, and may eventually result in rectal prolapse. If left to persist, the animal will become extremely dehydrated very quickly, and may die as a result. Diagnosis is by clinical examination and, although supportive care and therapy may ease the condition, treatment is rarely successful.

Pyometra

This is the accumulation of pus within the uterus, and is only occasionally seen in ferrets; when it does occur, it is immediately after the start of a pseudo-pregnancy. Organisms responsible for this condition in ferrets include *Streptococcus*, *Staphylococcus*, *E. coli*, and *Corynebacterium*. Affected ferrets will be anorexic, lethargic, and will often have a fever. Medical attention must be sought immediately, as the uterus may rupture, causing peritonitis, and an ovariohysterectomy will be required urgently.

Rabies

In countries where this disease is prevalent, ferrets can become infected. Clinical signs of the disease include lethargy, posterior paralysis and anxiety; recovery of infected ferrets is not unusual.

Rat-tail or Bottle-Brush Syndrome

Rat-tail or 'bottle-brush', syndrome is the term applied to a ferret suffering from the loss of all the hair on its tail. While some authorities maintain that this is sign of stress, most veterinary surgeons believe that it is caused by an imbalance of hormones. It almost always coincides with the spring moult, when the ferret is shedding its winter coat. It is believed that the hormone imbalance causes the ferret to shed too much fur on its tail; in almost 100 per cent of such cases, the hair grows back naturally when the ferret has its autumn moult. However, if there is *persistent* hair loss, starting at the base of the tail and gradually moving up the back and over the entire body, this may be a sign of endocrine alopecia (see 'Endocrine Alopecia' and 'Alopecia').

Ringworm (Dermatophytosis)

Although rare, this condition is occasionally seen in ferrets. It is always contracted by contact with an infected cat or, extremely rarely, dog. Caused by the fungus *Microsporum canis*, this disease is not caused by a worm, as many are led to believe by its name, but is a fungal infection. The condition manifests itself with hair loss and bald, scaly patches of skin. Home treatment is sometimes successful, but it is strongly recommended that veterinary advice is sought. As the condition is transmissible to man, it must be treated immediately (see also 'Mites' and 'Alopecia').

Sarcoptic Mange – See 'Mites'.

Scours – See 'Diarrhoea'.

Shock
Shock, which is an acute fall in blood pressure, is often evident after the ferret has been involved in an accident or has been injured; certain diseases can also cause this condition. It manifests itself with cool skin; pale lips and gums (due to the lack of circulation); faint, rapid pulse; and staring but unseeing eyes.

The victim must be kept warm and the blood circulation returned to normal as soon as possible. Massaging the ferret will help circulation, and wrapping it in a towel or blanket will help keep it warm. The affected animal should be kept quiet and warm, and veterinary treatment sought as soon as possible.

Skin Tumours (Neoplasma)
Skin tumours are common in ferrets, and surgery is necessary in all cases, and should be carried out as soon as possible. These tumours are, however, very difficult to eliminate, and frequently recur. Warts also occur on ferrets, and so it is vital that histopathology is used to confirm all diagnoses. Consult your veterinary surgeon if any animal develops lumps anywhere on its body. See also 'Cancer'.

The Staggers – See 'Posterior Paralysis'.

Thiamine Deficiency
If ferrets are fed a diet consisting of a large proportion of day-old chicks, raw fish or eggs (or a combination of any or all of these items), a thiamine deficiency is almost guaranteed. Symptoms include anorexia, lethargy, weakness of the hindquarters and convulsions. Injections of the vitamin B complex usually have a rapid effect, and recovery is usually total. Avoid this problem by supplying your ferrets with a proper diet. All cases of convulsions, paralysis or unusual behaviour should be referred to your veterinary surgeon.

Tuberculosis
Ferrets are susceptible to avian, bovine and human tuberculosis. Symptoms include paralysis of the limbs, diarrhoea and wasting of

the body. Almost always fatal, the disease is highly contagious; contact your veterinary surgeon at once if you suspect this condition in your ferrets.

Urolithiasis (Gall Stones)

Gall stones sometimes occur in ferrets and vary in size from a particle of sand to quite a large stone. Treatment consists of antibiotics, surgery and the use of special diets to dissolve the stone.

Zinc Toxicity

Ferrets cannot tolerate high levels of zinc, and may become ill through the use of galvanised feeding dishes or even by licking or biting cage bars. Symptoms include anaemia, lethargy and weakness of the hind legs; liver and kidney failure can quickly follow. All suspected cases should be referred to a veterinary surgeon as soon as possible, although there is no actual treatment, and affected animals are unlikely to recover. It is common for vets to advise euthanasia for affected ferrets to avoid undue suffering.

*   *   *

Administering Medication

When a veterinary surgeon has prescribed medication for a ferret, it must be administered regularly, and the full course of drugs given. With liquid medicine, this should be administered with a dropper or syringe (obviously *without* a needle attached). The end of the pipette or syringe should be placed slowly in the side of the mouth, without using force. The medicine is slowly expelled into the ferret's mouth, allowing the animal time to swallow all of the medicine. If too much liquid is put in the ferret's mouth, there is a great risk of medication inhalation, leading to the development of a life-threatening lung infection.

Be warned; most ferrets do not like the taste of some liquid medications, and will shake their heads vigorously after treatment, splashing the liquid around. It is a wise precaution to administer such medications out-of-doors, and for the person dispensing the medication to wear an overall.

Where tablets or pills are prescribed, it may be possible to administer the pill by hiding it in a treat item, such as a lump of meat. Some owners cover the tablet in fat, or some other tasty covering; neither of these methods is foolproof. Alternatively, the tablets can be pushed to the back of the ferret's mouth, to the edge of the throat. By stroking the ferret's neck, the animal can be encouraged to swallow the pill. Some vets and pet shops sell 'Pet pillers', which are another alternative that can work.

* * *

In many cases, health problems are avoidable, and the best way to ensure healthy ferrets is to indulge in good husbandry, including the provision of an adequate balanced diet. Ferrets have the disturbing habit of often not showing any symptoms until they are almost dead. If you suspect any of your stock of 'sickening', contact your veterinary surgeon without delay; time waited is time wasted.

CHAPTER ELEVEN

FIRST AID

The Basics of First Aid

First aid is the skilled application of accepted principles of treatment, on the occurrence of an accident, or in the case of a sudden illness, using facilities and materials available at the time. The objectives of first aid are threefold:

- To sustain life
- To prevent the patient's condition worsening
- To promote the patient's recovery

When finding an injured ferret, you should:

a. Assess the situation
b. Diagnose the condition
c. Treat immediately and adequately

Assessing the Situation

Keep calm, and look at what has happened/is happening. While it is imperative that time is not wasted, it is just as important that you do not act hastily and, in so doing, make matters worse. Wherever possible, the cause of the animal's pain and distress should be taken away from the animal, rather than the animal being moved from the pain.

Look for any indications as to the cause of the ferret's problem. Signs to look for include:

- State of consciousness
- Breathing
- Bleeding
- Fractures
- Shock

- Movement
- Pain

Your priorities must be:

AIRWAYS
BREATHING
CIRCULATION

In other words, if the patient is not breathing, get the airways clear before you try to get the animal breathing, and only once the animal is breathing should you concern yourself with the heart and/or bleeding. Airways can be blocked by a foreign body, or it could be that the ferret's tongue is blocking its throat. Vomit is another major cause of blocked airways.

Once the airways are clear, check that the ferret is breathing. Very often, once the airways are clear, the animal will recommence breathing without any help. If the ferret does not start breathing once the airways are cleared, then you must take immediate action, otherwise the animal will die. Artificial respiration, though difficult, is possible with ferrets. If a ferret has stopped breathing, rather than give mouth-to-mouth respiration, hold the ferret by its hind legs and, keeping your arms straight, swing the animal to left and then to right. This transfers the weight of the ferret's internal organs on and off the diaphragm, causing the lungs to fill and empty of air. Keep this up until the ferret begins breathing on its own, until help arrives, or until you believe the ferret is beyond help.

If the ferret is not conscious, you should next check that the ferret's heart is beating. This is best achieved by placing your ear against the animal's chest and listening intently. Such a small animal has only a small heart, and consequently the sounds of the heart will be very difficult to hear. A stethoscope is an obvious advantage here, but it is unlikely that, in a first aid situation, one will always be to hand. An indication of the ferret's heart beat is the colour of the mucous membranes inside the animal's mouth. If the animal's heart is beating normally, then its blood circulation will be normal, and the gums should be pink. If the gums are pale or white, this could indicate a serious circulation problem, such as internal bleeding, heart failure or shock. If, on the other hand, the gums are bright red, this could indicate toxaemia (an overwhelming systemic infection) – a potentially serious condition.

If you are certain that the ferret's heart has stopped, lay the animal on its left hand side and apply *gentle* pressure to its rib cage. You will feel the rib cage move about 10 mm (½ in); do not push and never go beyond 10 mm. Release the pressure; this is one cycle. Repeat a cycle about every couple of seconds. Once the ferret is breathing, if it does not return to consciousness, ensure that you keep a check on its breathing while, at the same time, checking for other injuries.

If the ferret is unconscious and bleeding from its ears, nose or mouth, try to keep the animal horizontal and immobilised, and do not move the animal more than you have to. Such symptoms could indicate cervical (neck) injuries, which often occur at the same time as injuries to the head; if the ferret is suffering such injuries, too much movement may result in permanent injury or paralysis.

While attending the ferret, take note of its breathing; is it fast or slow? Is it smooth and easy or laboured? Check the pupils; are they dilated or very small? Are the animal's muscles supple or stiff? Is the ferret responsive to voices and/or touch? All such information will help the veterinary surgeon treat the animal's injuries, and could save its life. Remember to ensure your own safety at all times.

First Aid Kit
Some of the most common ferret injuries – minor cuts and abrasions – occur when the animal is going about its daily routine, or is being worked. It is important that injuries are treated as soon as possible, in order to minimise adverse effects. A small first aid kit should therefore be kept in the building housing the ferrets, and one should also be taken along on every outing. Of course, you must have the necessary skill and experience to treat these minor injuries. If there is any doubt as to the seriousness of the injuries, or the ferret's general condition, veterinary treatment should be sought as soon as it is practical.

A suitable first aid kit for ferrets should contain the following items as a minimum, and should always accompany you on any field trip, and be near at hand at all times.

1. NAIL CLIPPERS
These should be top quality, and can be used for trimming the ferret's nails. Use the type that work on the guillotine principle, where one blade hits the other, rather than on the scissors principle,

which can result in nails being pulled out. Ferrets' nails should not be cut too often and never trimmed too short; leave about 3–5 mm beyond the quick.

2. TWEEZERS
For the removal of foreign bodies, stings etc.

3. SCISSORS
These should be curved and round-ended, and should be used to cut off the fur around any wound. They must *not* be used for trimming nails. When trimming fur, dip the blades in water before cutting; the cut fur will adhere to the blades, and can be rinsed off in the water before making the next cut, thus eliminating the risk of hairs falling into wounds.

4. ANTISEPTIC LOTION
For cleansing cuts, wounds and abrasions. Lotions for humans are just as effective on ferrets, and can be obtained from any pharmacist's shop.

5. ANTISEPTIC POWDER
Should be applied to wounds after they have been thoroughly cleansed. It serves to dry the wound, cleanse it and prevent ingress of dirt etc., as well as aiding the healing process.

6. ANTISEPTIC OINTMENT
Antiseptic ointment can be used instead of antiseptic powder. We use an ointment that is coloured a vivid green, which helps to indicate to everyone exactly where the wound is.

7. ANTIHISTAMINE CREAM
Occasionally, a ferret will be stung by a bee, wasp or other such insect that has managed to find its way into its cage. The sting should be removed with tweezers, and antihistamine cream applied.

8. COTTON WOOL
Used for cleaning wounds, cuts and abrasions, and for stemming the flow of blood. Ensure it is kept in airtight containers to prevent soiling.

9. SURGICAL GAUZE
Used for padding wounds and stemming the flow of blood. This is supplied in sterile packaging; once opened, any surplus gauze must not be used for wound dressing etc., as it will no longer be sterile.

10. ADHESIVE PLASTERS
Although these will soon be chewed off by the ferret, they are useful for applying directly to small wounds and for keeping dressings in place. They can also be used for minor splinting. Keep a range of sizes, remembering that large plasters can be cut to size, whereas small ones cannot be enlarged.

11. BANDAGES
Small bandages should be kept for binding broken limbs and wounds. They will, of course, be temporary, as the ferret will chew them off. Again, a selection of suitable sizes should be in the first aid kit.

12. COTTON BUDS
Ideal for cleaning wounds and applying ointments etc. With care, they can also be used to clean the pinnae (ear flaps) but *under no circumstances* should you poke these (or any other object) down the ear canal.

13. TABLE SALT
A solution of table salt – two teaspoons of salt to 0.5 litres (1 pint) of water – is good for washing debris from wounds and countering infection. When applying such a solution, it can be drizzled/poured onto the wound to wash out debris; it is also excellent for washing out eyes. Take care that the contaminated solution does not flow into other wounds, or into healthy eyes.

14. SODIUM BICARBONATE
On a wet compress, this will help to reduce swelling. It can also be used to reduce the effect of bee stings.

15. VINEGAR
This common household fluid can be used to reduce the effect of wasp stings.

15. ALCOHOL (SURGICAL SPIRIT)
Useful for the removal of ticks etc.

16. STYPTIC PENCIL
Sold in human pharmacies, and made from aluminium sulphate, one of these will help to stem the flow of blood from wounds. Beware, however, that styptic pencils sting on application to an open wound, and the ferret may well react by biting the hands holding the animal.

17. RECTAL THERMOMETER
To take the ferret's temperature. We favour the electronic type, although the 'old fashioned' spirit/mercury filled glass thermometers are still popular and effective (see 'Taking a Ferret's Temperature' page 211.)

18. STETHOSCOPE
To check for the ferret's heartbeat. These instruments are not particularly expensive, but users need some basic training in their use. Ask your veterinary surgeon to show you how to use one, and to help identify the different sounds heard through this instrument, which can also be used to listen to the sound of lungs, the stomach and other parts of the ferret's internal workings.

19. HYPODERMIC SYRINGES
This item is essential for administering liquid medication orally. Keep a range of sizes in the kit.

Many of the items listed can be used on both ferret and human injuries, and most are available from pharmacies and pet shops. Specialised items can be obtained from veterinary practices. Where items of equipment are involved, it is vital that the user has experience of these items *before* they are needed in an emergency situation. At such times, stress levels in first aiders are high, and having to work out how to use a piece of equipment will do nothing to reduce these levels. Similarly, artificial respiration and such 'simple' procedures as bandaging should be practised before they are needed to be used on a sick or injured animal.

Bites and Stings
These are split into four categories – insect, snake, rat and ferret.

INSECT BITES (INCLUDING STINGS)
Clip a little fur away from the area, so that you can actually see the problem, then wash with saline solution. Bees leave their sting in the victim, whereas wasps do not. If there is a sting present, it should be carefully removed with the tweezers and then the area wiped with cotton wool (or a cotton bud) soaked in alcohol, such as surgical spirit. For wasp stings, a little vinegar will prove beneficial, while for bee stings, use a little bicarbonate of soda. Dry the area thoroughly, and use an antihistamine spray or apply a wet compress to help reduce the irritation and swelling.

If the ferret has been bitten or stung in the throat, veterinary attention must be sought as soon as possible; such stings can cause swelling that may block the airways and thus kill the ferret.

RAT BITES
Rat bites are one of the most dangerous bites that a ferret may suffer; they are quite common in working ferrets (i.e. those used for hunting rabbits and rats). Rats can carry many harmful diseases and so it is essential that no risks are taken. If you suspect that a ferret has been bitten by a rat, you can safely assume that there will be rat urine in the area and even on the ferret. As rats carry leptospirosis, a disease that is potentially fatal to humans, and this is spread via the rat's urine, you should use protective gloves when handling the ferret, and bathe the animal to remove all rat urine. Affected carryboxes and cages should also be cleaned with a top quality disinfectant.

Clip away the fur from around the wound, ensuring that the clippings do not become entangled in the wound itself. Wetting the scissors is recommended, as the hairs stick to the blades rather than falling onto the wound; dipping the scissors into a dish of water after each snip will remove all hairs from the metal. Thoroughly clean the area of the wound with a saline solution and then an antiseptic liquid; dry and apply liberal amounts of antiseptic dusting powder. If the wound is large, or you have good reason to believe that the rat was infected, take the injured ferret to a veterinary surgeon as soon as possible after the injury, where the vet may well administer an injection of antibiotics. I would always recommend this action after any rat bite – it is better to be safe than sorry.

SNAKE BITES
In the UK, we have only one species of venomous snake, the adder (*Vipera berus*), sometimes referred to as the viper, while in some other countries, there are several species of venomous snake. Under normal circumstances, it is unusual for ferrets or dogs to be bitten by these reptiles. During the cooler temperatures of spring or early summer, the snakes are rather lethargic, especially the gravid (pregnant) females. At such times, they will keep still as long as possible, even when approached. If your ferret or dog does not see the snake and stands on it, the snake will bite. If your animal is bitten by a snake, it is most important that you keep the injured animal as calm as possible (and you must also remain calm, as your actions will influence the animal), and seek immediate veterinary attention.

FERRET BITES
Although it may seem strange, ferrets are more likely to suffer from bites from other ferrets than from any other animal. This is especially the case during the breeding season, when the hob takes hold of the jill by the scruff, hanging on tightly and, very often, breaking the jill's skin with his teeth. While often looking very bad, these types of injuries are not usually serious, providing that they are given first aid treatment as soon as possible.

The area of the bite must be clipped of fur, and the wound thoroughly washed with a saline solution followed by an antiseptic liquid. A good dusting with an antiseptic wound powder will finish the job. If action is not taken, the wound may fester and result in abscesses.

Bleeding
Never apply tourniquets (see 'Cuts, Abrasions and Other Wounds').

Breathing Problems
Ferrets gasping for breath are obviously showing symptoms of some form of breathing difficulty; this may be heatstroke (see 'Heatstroke'), fluid on the lungs or an obstruction of some kind. Many obstructions can easily be removed from a ferret's mouth

with a cotton bud or even a finger, but take care that the stressed animal does not bite you as you are trying to help it.

Artificial respiration, though difficult, is possible with ferrets. If a ferret has stopped breathing, rather than give mouth-to-mouth respiration, hold the ferret by its hind legs and, keeping your arms straight, swing the animal to the left and then to the right. This transfers the weight of the ferret's internal organs on and off the diaphragm, causing the lungs to fill and empty of air. Keep this up until the ferret begins breathing on its own, until help arrives, or until you believe the ferret to be beyond help.

Convulsions

Convulsions are a symptom, an indication that the ferret has an infection of some kind or has been poisoned, and *not* a disease *per se*. There are obviously many possible causes for convulsions, and one of the most common in captive ferrets is heatstroke, or 'the sweats'. However, if your ferret is suffering from convulsions, you should seek urgent veterinary attention.

Cuts, Abrasions and Other Wounds

There are several different types of wound that a ferret may suffer, and each requires a slightly different technique.

INCISED (CLEAN) CUT

These are straight cuts, as one would get from a sharp knife blade; as such, they bleed profusely. This bleeding, which can be very frightening to people not used to such things (a little blood appears as 'gallons' to many lay people, even though there may only be a thimble-full) helps clear the wound of debris, and thus lessens the possibility of infection.

Bleeding should be stemmed by direct pressure, if at all possible; where it is not, apply indirect pressure on an artery at the heart side of the wound. Elevating the injury will enable gravity to help reduce the blood flow. Apply a suitable dressing; large and/or deep cuts will almost certainly require sutures (stitches) from a veterinary surgeon.

LACERATED CUTS

These are tears in the skin, as caused by barbed wire, for instance, and such injuries will bleed less profusely than incised cuts. The big danger with lacerations is that the injury will have pushed dirt and debris into the wound, and the lack of bleeding will mean that the dirt is not washed out. You must clean the wound with a saline solution (two teaspoons of salt to half a litre (1 pint) of warm water); dry the wound and the surrounding area, and apply a dressing if necessary.

CONTUSION (BRUISE)

This is a sign of internal bleeding, and a careful watch must be kept on the injured animal. Bruises on furred animals such as ferrets are difficult to see, but if the animal has been in a fall or similar accident, the fur should be blown apart and the skin will then become more visible. Also, a ferret with bruises is likely to be tender in those areas, and will wince when handled. For minor bruising, there is little action that can be taken, but the animal should be observed regularly, and if its condition causes concern, a veterinary surgeon should be consulted. If shock sets in, seek veterinary advice immediately.

PUNCTURE (STAB)

Puncture wounds, which can be caused by nails, slivers of wood and other such objects, usually appear very small at the surface but, of course, could be very deep. *Never* remove any object from a wound, as this may aggravate the injury and/or allow large amounts of bleeding. Apply pressure around the wound site, using a dressing to maintain the pressure, and seek immediate veterinary attention. Deep wounds can cause other complications – shock, unconsciousness, heart failure etc. – and so the affected animal should be taken to the veterinary surgeon without delay.

GUNSHOT WOUNDS

If you work (hunt with) your ferret, then it is possible that it may be accidentally shot. The most common type of wound to a working ferret is from a shotgun, in which case the animal will be peppered with balls of shot, which will all require removal; bleeding should not be profuse. The other type of wound is from a single projectile, i.e. a bullet. Bullets make two wounds – one in (entry wound) and one out (exit wound). Where 'sporting' (hollow point) ammunition is used, the exit wound will be several times larger than the entry wound.

In all cases of gunshot wound, stem the flow of blood, keep the animal calm, checking for signs of trauma, and seek veterinary treatment immediately.

Fractures

Fractures are caused by either direct or indirect pressure on the bones, which may crack or break. Where the bone is broken and pierces the skin, this is known as an open or compound fracture, and all other such injuries as closed fractures. Signs of fracture are usually obvious – painful movement of the limb, tenderness, swelling, loss of control of the limb, deformity of the limb, unnatural movement of the limb, and crepitus (the sensation or, in very bad cases, the sound of the two ends of the bones grinding on each other). A ferret with a fractured bone will be in pain, and may not take kindly to being handled. Care should therefore be taken to avoid being bitten by the injured ferret.

Keep the injured ferret quiet, and steady and support the injured limb, immobilising it with bandages and splints if necessary, to prevent it moving and causing greater damage. Wrapping the injured animal in a piece of Vetbed, fleece, towelling or a blanket will help immobilise the limb and keep the ferret quiet and restrained. Raising the limb will help reduce discomfort and swelling (by reducing the blood flow). Veterinary attention must be sought for all fractures.

Heatstroke (The Sweats)

Ferrets react adversely to too much heat, and if left in such conditions for a long period, may well die from heatstroke. This affliction is often referred to as 'the sweats', which is a very misleading term, since ferrets cannot sweat. As in all things, prevention is better than cure. Never site the ferrets' cage in direct sunlight, and never leave a ferret unattended in a car. A ferret should also not be transported in such a manner that the animal or its carrying box is in full sunlight while in the car.

In extreme summer temperatures, or in areas where it is known that the temperature will be high, every effort must be made to insulate the ferrets' cage, and place it in an area where it and its inmates are protected from the full effect of varying temperatures. Where it is not possible to keep the ferrets' cage as cool as one would like, wet cloths may be hung over the cage to keep the temperature down,

208

although these cloths will soon dry out, and so they will require constant attention throughout the day. Placing bricks on each corner of the cage roof, and then positioning a piece of timber over them, will act as 'double glazing', and will be extremely effective in reducing heat build-up in the cage. Where ferret cages are kept in a building, the building itself should be insulated and well ventilated. Opening doors and windows in extremely high temperatures will help reduce the build-up of heat in the building. All opening doors and windows should be fitted with secure netting-covered frames to prevent the ingress of animals and humans.

The first sign of heatstroke or heat exhaustion is an agitated ferret in obvious distress. If in its cage, the affected ferret will stretch out and pant heavily; if left untreated, it will eventually collapse, pass into a coma and die. Immediately a ferret shows symptoms of heatstroke, you must act – and fast; delay can be fatal. The ferret's body is overheating, and so your first task must be to lower its body temperature. With mildly affected ferrets, simply moving them to a cool area, and ensuring a steady passage of cool air over them, is usually effective; a light spraying with cold water from a plant mister is beneficial, as is the use of an electric fan to improve the flow of air over the affected animal. Such a fan must be placed so that the ferret cannot come into contact with it. In bad cases, where it is literally make or break, we find that the best method is to immerse the animal to the neck in a bucket of cold water, repeating this procedure regularly for the next few minutes, by which time the ferret should be showing signs of recovery. Ensure that the ferret is thoroughly dried, and placed in a cage in a cool area, with a small amount of hay for bedding; this hay will also help to dry the ferret's coat. This is a very drastic treatment, and should only be attempted when the animal is very badly affected, and where to delay further will lead to the animal's death.

In all cases, it is vital to keep the affected animal's head cool, since brain death can occur, as the brain is quite literally cooked. In all but mild cases, veterinary advice should be sought for the animal at the earliest opportunity.

Hypothermia
Hypothermia, an abnormally low body temperature, can be fatal to ferrets. In cases of significant hypothermia, the ferret will become physically and mentally sluggish, with severe hypothermia; the

animal is likely to become unconscious. It is essential, if a ferret shows symptoms of hypothermia, that the animal is warmed slowly. If hypothermia besets a ferret while you are in the field, wrap a 'space blanket', towel or human garment around the animal to try to keep it warm. A small heat pack can be placed close to the afflicted ferret, but should never be placed on the animal, as localised heat can cause problems. Veterinary treatment must be given to the afflicted ferret, as soon as practicable.

Poisoning

The ingesting of substances that are harmful can be fatal; ferrets allowed free roam of a human home are probably most at risk, although any ferret may come into contact with poisonous materials. Such materials include:

- Antifreeze (ethylene glycol) – ferrets and other animals like this because of the sweet taste
- Motor oil or other petroleum products
- Plants – both house plants and garden plants can be toxic to ferrets. Although ferrets are carnivorous and so highly unlikely to eat vegetation, the following common plants are toxic (poisonous) to ferrets – rhododendron, laburnum, hemlock, ragwort, laurel, foxglove
- Rat poison or insecticides
- Detergents or cleaning agents

Some of these substances, but not all, have antidotes. However, before any treatment can begin, it is vital that full details of exactly what the ferret has ingested must be ascertained. If you suspect a ferret has been poisoned, make every effort to find out exactly what the ferret has ingested, but do not delay seeking veterinary advice.

Shock

Shock is an acute fall in blood pressure, and is often seen when a ferret has been involved in an accident or has been injured in some way. The condition manifests itself with cool skin, and pale lips and gums (due to the lack of circulation); an affected ferret will have a faint and rapid pulse, and its eyes will be staring but unseeing.

In all cases of severe shock, the victim must be kept warm and the ferret gently massaged to help the blood circulation return to normal as soon as possible. Wrap an affected ferret in a piece of

Vetbed, a towel or a piece of human clothing, such as a sweater, to help keep the animal warm. The ferret should be kept quiet and warm, and veterinary treatment sought as soon as practical.

Taking a Ferret's Temperature

Shake down the thermometer, and coat it with a lubricant such as K-Y Jelly or petroleum jelly (e.g. Vaseline). This is a two-person procedure, and one person should hold the ferret firmly, while the other gently and slowly inserts the thermometer about 10 mm (½ inch) into the animal's rectum. The thermometer should be held in place for about a minute, at which time it can be removed and read. The ferret's normal temperature is 38.6°C, with a range of 37.8–40°C.

Moving an Injured Ferret

When a ferret is so badly injured that it cannot move, it will need to be carried. To do this, the ferret should be wrapped gently in a bulky material such as Vetbed. If this is not available, a towel, pillowcase, or a fleece will suffice. Whatever material you use, ensure that all of the ferret's body (except its head) is inside the wrap; the head should be fully exposed to allow the ferret to breathe easily. In all such cases when a ferret is so badly injured, seek veterinary attention immediately.

Emergency and Convalescence Feed

When an animal is injured, or convalescing from an illness, its appetite may not be good, and it will need to be tempted to feed by giving it a food that is highly palatable, easy digestible and highly nutritious. While there are such foods available for cats and dogs, there are no such commercial feeds for ferrets. Over the years, we have developed a food that serves the purpose admirably, and is easily put together by the average ferret breeder. We call it 'Ferret Recupe', and the recipe is set out below.

- 1 x 57 g (2½ oz) pack of chicken-flavoured Complan convalescence food
- 200 ml (8 fluid oz) of kitten milk substitute
- 100 g (4 oz) of top quality dry complete ferret food (we use Ferret Complete – James Wellbeloved, England)
- Electrolyte solution

- ½ tsp Brewer's yeast powder (or one crushed brewer's yeast tablet)
- ½ tsp SA 30 (multivitamins and minerals)

METHOD

Soak the complete ferret food in enough warm electrolyte solution (see Chapter 10) to cover and soften the feed completely. Reconstitute the Complan, and pour in with the softened ferret food. Add the kitten milk substitute, half a teaspoon of brewer's yeast (or one crushed brewer's yeast tablet), and half a teaspoon of SA 30. Mix the contents thoroughly (we use a blender) until it is the consistency of soft ice cream. When thoroughly mixed, the feed is ready to give to the ailing ferret. We also make up a mix of this, and then freeze small amounts in ice cube trays and small margarine containers, for later use. Sick or injured ferrets should be given small amounts – warmed – several times daily, to aid their recuperation and recovery. When a ferret is too ill to take this semi-solid feed, we give them reconstituted Complan (warm), via a syringe.

APPENDIX ONE

PARTURITION CALENDAR

By adjusting the photoperiod under which ferrets are kept (as detailed elsewhere), it is possible to breed ferrets throughout the year. Consequently, this parturition table covers all year. To use the table, simply look in the columns marked 'DATE MATED', and then across to the adjacent column marked 'DATE DUE' to find the expected date of the birth of the litter resulting from the mating. Remember that litters can be born a few days either side of this date, as the gestation of the ferret varies from forty to forty-four days.

Very young kits in their nest.

DATE MATED JAN	DATE DUE FEB	DATE MATED FEB	DATE DUE MARCH	DATE MATED MARCH	DATE DUE APRIL	DATE MATED APRIL	DATE DUE MAY	DATE MATED MAY	DATE DUE JUNE	DATE MATED JUNE	DATE DUE JULY
1	11	1	14	1	11	1	12	1	11	1	12
2	12	2	15	2	12	2	13	2	12	2	13
3	13	3	16	3	13	3	14	3	13	3	14
4	14	4	17	4	14	4	15	4	14	4	15
5	15	5	18	5	15	5	16	5	15	5	16
6	16	6	19	6	16	6	17	6	16	6	17
7	17	7	20	7	17	7	18	7	17	7	18
8	18	8	21	8	18	8	19	8	18	8	19
9	19	9	22	9	19	9	20	9	19	9	20
10	20	10	23	10	20	10	21	10	20	10	21
11	21	11	24	11	21	11	22	11	21	11	22
12	22	12	25	12	22	12	23	12	22	12	23
13	23	13	26	13	23	13	24	13	23	13	24
14	24	14	27	14	24	14	25	14	24	14	25
15	25	15	28	15	25	15	26	15	25	15	26
16	26	16	29	16	26	16	27	16	26	16	27
17	27	17	30	17	27	17	28	17	27	17	28
18	28	18	31	18	28	18	29	18	28	18	29
19	MARCH 1	19	APRIL 1	19	29	19	30	19	29	19	30
20	2	20	2	20	30	20	31	20	30	20	31
21	3	21	3	21	MAY 1	21	JUNE 1	21	JULY 1	21	AUGUST 1
22	4	22	4	22	2	22	2	22	2	22	2
23	5	23	5	23	3	23	3	23	3	23	3
24	6	24	6	24	4	24	4	24	4	24	4
25	7	25	7	25	5	25	5	25	5	25	5
26	8	26	8	26	6	26	6	26	6	26	6
27	9	27	9	27	7	27	7	27	7	27	7
28	10	28	10	28	8	28	8	28	8	28	8
29	11			29	9	29	9	29	9	29	9
30	12			30	10	30	10	30	10	30	10
31	13			31	11			31	11		

DATE MATED JULY	DATE DUE AUGUST	DATE MATED AUGUST	DATE DUE SEP	DATE MATED SEP	DATE DUE OCT	DATE MATED OCT	DATE DUE NOV	DATE MATED NOV	DATE DUE DEC	DATE MATED DEC	DATE DUE JAN
1	11	1	11	1	12	1	11	1	12	1	11
2	12	2	12	2	13	2	12	2	13	2	12
3	13	3	13	3	14	3	13	3	14	3	13
4	14	4	14	4	15	4	14	4	15	4	14
5	15	5	15	5	16	5	15	5	16	5	15
6	16	6	16	6	17	6	16	6	17	6	16
7	17	7	17	7	18	7	17	7	18	7	17
8	18	8	18	8	19	8	18	8	19	8	18
9	19	9	19	9	20	9	19	9	20	9	19
10	20	10	20	10	21	10	20	10	21	10	20
11	21	11	21	11	22	11	21	11	22	11	21
12	22	12	22	12	23	12	22	12	23	12	22
13	23	13	23	13	24	13	23	13	24	13	23
14	24	14	24	14	25	14	24	14	25	14	24
15	25	15	25	15	26	15	25	15	26	15	25
16	26	16	26	16	27	16	26	16	27	16	26
17	27	17	27	17	28	17	27	17	28	17	27
18	28	18	28	18	29	18	28	18	29	18	28
19	29	19	29	19	30	19	29	19	30	19	29
20	30	20	30	20	31	20	30	20	31	20	30
21	31	21	OCT 1	21	NOV 1	21	DEC 1	21	JAN 1	21	31
22	SEP 1	22	2	22	2	22	2	22	2	22	FEB 1
23	2	23	3	23	3	23	3	23	3	23	2
24	3	24	4	24	4	24	4	24	4	24	3
25	4	25	5	25	5	25	5	25	5	25	4
26	5	26	6	26	6	26	6	26	6	26	5
27	6	27	7	27	7	27	7	27	7	27	6
28	7	28	8	28	8	28	8	28	8	28	7
29	8	29	9	29	9	29	9	29	9	29	8
30	9	30	10	30	10	30	10	30	10	30	9
31	10	31	11			31	11			31	10

APPENDIX TWO

FERRET FACTS AND FIGURES

Average weight (adult)	Between 400 g (14 oz) and 2 kg (4.4 lb)
Average size (adult)	Between 35 and 60 cm (14–24 in) (hob up to twice size of jill)
Average lifespan (in captivity)	Between 8 and 12 years; ferrets of 14 years have been recorded
Age at puberty	250 days (approx.)
Age at sexual maturity	8 to 12 months (spring after birth)
Normal breeding season (Britain)	Early March to late September
Number of chromosomes	40 (20 pairs), i.e. N = 20
Breeding season	Triggered by photoperiod – require longer days than nights
First possible mating	6 months
Duration of oestrus	Ceases when mated; if unmated, will continue to end of 'season', causing potential medical problems
Signs of oestrus	Vulva swells, becomes vivid pink colour, secretion. In male, testes swell and descend into scrotum
Duration of mating	Several hours
Ovulation	About 30 hours after coitus (mating)
Reduction of vulva	Begins 7–10 days after mating, complete within 2–3 weeks
Palpation	10 days after vulva totally reduced
Gestation (pregnancy)	40–44 days; average 42 days
Number of young (in one litter)	2–15 (average 6–8). Jills can have up to four litters per year. Largest litter recorded – 18

Litters per year	Under normal conditions 1 or 2; with extra lighting (i.e. adjustment of photoperiod) up to 4
Post-natal oestrus	1–2 weeks after weaning
Weight at birth	5–15 g (up to ½ oz)
State at birth	Altricial – i.e. blind, deaf, naked and entirely dependent upon the mother
Ears open	32 days
Eyes open	32–5 days
Fur	In dark-coloured kits, starts to appear within 5–7 days. Good covering by 4 weeks
Deciduous teeth	Begin to erupt at about 14 days; all showing by 18 days
Permanent canine teeth	47–52 days
Shedding of deciduous canine teeth	56 – 70 days
Movement	Kits as young as 2–3 weeks will manage to crawl out of nest (to be dragged back by the mother)
Weaning	6–7 weeks
Weight at weaning	300–500 g (10–18 oz)
Age attain adult weight/size	4–5 months
Minimum selling/buying age	10 weeks
Rectal temperature	38.6° C (range 37.8–40°C)
Heart rate	220–250 bpm
Respiratory rate	30–40 per minute
Number of digits (toes)	5 per foot
Teeth	Incisors 3/3, canines 1/1, premolars 3/3, molars 1/2. Supernumerary incisors not uncommon
Nipples	2 rows of 4 (8 in total) – on both sexes
Vertebrae	7 cervical, 14 thoracic, 6 lumbar, 3 sacral, 14–18 coccygeal or caudal, 14–15 pairs of ribs (some ferrets have fourteen ribs on one side, and fifteen on the other)

Other anatomy   No appendix, or caecum. Under-
                                    developed sweat glands

Sexing   Ano-genital distance of the jill is
                                    half that of the hob

Optimum ambient temperature   22°C (72°F)

GLOSSARY OF
TECHNICAL TERMS

Acute A medical condition with severe signs and a short duration.

Agalactia The partial or complete lack of milk despite no disease of the mammary gland.

Allele The alternative form of a genetic locus; a single allele for each locus is inherited separately from each parent.

Androgens The male sex hormones.

Ano-genital distance The distance between the animal's anus and its genital opening.

Anophthalmic Eyeless.

Anthrozoonotic A disease capable of being passed from humans to animals; a prime example for the ferret is influenza (the flu), which can kill young, old or weak ferrets.

Antibacterial A synthetic drug that has the ability to kill or inhibit the growth of microorganisms.

Antibiotic A drug originally derived from a living organism, which has the ability to kill or inhibit the growth of micro-organisms.

Aspirate The withdrawal of fluid by negative pressure or suction.

Asymptomatic Without symptoms.

Autosome A chromosome that is not one of the sex chromosomes.

Bacterium/Bacteria A single cell micro-organism that lacks a true nucleus.

Baculum The J-shaped bone in a hob's penis; it is thought that it helps the penis act as a vaginal stop, keeping semen from leaking out before fertilising the jill's ova.

Benign Neither malignant nor recurrent, and therefore recovery is likely.

Biopsy The taking of a small piece of affected tissue for laboratory analysis.

Canine Distemper (CD) See 'Distemper, Canine'.

Canines The large, sharp, curved teeth that are located on each side of the ferret's mouth. Also referred to as eye teeth.

Carbohydrates Food constituents, including sugar and starch, that are an important source of energy.

Carcinogenic Cancer-causing agent.

Carrier An animal that has a pathogen to which it is immune but that it can pass on to other animals.

Cartilage Gristly connective tissue.

Castration The surgical removal of a hob's testes, i.e. neutering. A castrated hob is known as a hobble.

Cauterise To 'seal' a wound or similar using heat or chemicals.

Chromosome Components of a cell that contain genetic information, with every chromosome containing numerous genes.

Chronic A disease that persists for a long time.

Co-dominance The situation in which both alleles in a heterozygous individual are expressed, so that the phenotype of the heterozygote incorporates the phenotypic effect of each allele.

Coitus The physical act of mating.

Colostrum The thin, white, first milk produced by the jill's mammary glands during late pregnancy and for a few days after childbirth. It provides the kits with essential nutrients and infection-fighting antibodies.

Congenital Present at birth and throughout the life of the animal concerned.

Cope A muzzle.

Cross A heterozygote, or the result of a mating of a ferret and a (true) polecat.

Crossing-over The process whereby parts of maternal and paternal chromosomes are exchanged, resulting in a 'shuffling' of alleles.

Cryptorchid A male with no testes descended into his scrotum.

Dam The mother of a litter.

Database A collection of data; can be computer-based or held on paper.

Dehydration A condition caused by the loss of too much fluid from the body. Severe diarrhoea or vomiting can cause dehydration.

De-musk See 'De-scent'.

De-scent To surgically remove the scent glands; in the UK such operations are unethical, except where there are medical reasons for the operation.

Deleterious Bad.

Di-hybrid inheritance Two differing attributes acquired via biological heredity from the parents.

Diploid i.e. 2N (in the ferret, N = 20). See also 'Haploid'

Distemper, Canine An infectious disease of ferrets (and also dogs, as the name implies).

Diuretic A drug to increase the production of urine in an animal.

Dominant The 'strong' allele, i.e. one that produces the same phenotype whether its paired allele is identical or different.

Dystocia A jill's inability to give birth.

Ectoparasite A parasite that lives on the outside of the host animal e.g. fleas, lice and ticks. See also 'Parasite' and 'Endoparasite'.

Electrolyte A substance to replace vital elements lost when an animal's water intake is reduced, i.e. when the animal is dehydrated. It is a mixture of salts in solution (i.e. dissolved in water). Sometimes referred to as 'rehydrating fluid'.

Endoparasite A parasite that lives inside the host animal, (e.g. in the intestines etc.), such as tapeworms. See also 'Parasite' and 'Ectoparasite'.

Endoscope An instrument for allowing a vet to look into body cavities.

Epistasis The masking of the effects of one gene by the action of another.

Euthanasia The humane killing of a ferret.

F1, F2 etc. F is short-hand for 'filial', a word derived from the Latin *filius* (son). Breeders use the term F1 to indicate the first generation offspring from a specific mating, with F2 for the second generation, F3 for the third, *et al.*

Fancy The term applied to the keeping and exhibition of animals.

Fancy animal An animal kept and bred to a standard for exhibition.

Fats Food constituents that are an important source of energy. A surplus of fats in a ferret's diet will cause it to become overweight, and will endanger its health, especially if it does not get sufficient exercise.

Fibre The indigestible material present in some foods that helps stimulate the action of the intestines. Used to be known as 'roughage'.

Fungicide Drugs that destroy fungi or fungal infections.

Gametes Sex cells, i.e. ova or sperm.

Gender The sex of an animal.

Gangrene The death of body tissue, associated with the loss of the blood supply to that tissue.

Gene A hereditary factor of inherited material. Genes are carried on chromosomes.

Gene interaction The collaboration of several different genes in the production of one phenotypic character or related group of characters.

Gene pool The total number of alleles available among reproductive members of a breeding population.

Genetics The study of the ways in which certain characteristics are passed on from one generation to the next.

Genitals (genitalia) The external sex organs of a ferret.

Genome The complete set of genetic information of an organism.

Genotype The genetic make up of a ferret.

Germ cell The egg of a jill, and the sperm of the hob.

Gestation Pregnancy. In ferrets, this is between 41 and 43 days, usually 42.

Gonad An organ that produces gametes (ova and sperm), i.e., an ovary or a testis.

Haematology The study of the ferret's blood, usually to help diagnose a disease.

Haploid i.e. N (in the ferret, N = 20). Se also 'Diploid'.

Heat A term often used to describe oestrus.

Heatstroke The effect of too much heat on a ferret. If this condition is not treated, it can be fatal. Sometimes referred to as 'the sweats'.

Helminths Parasitic worms.

Hernia A protrusion of part of the ferret's organs through an abnormal opening in the surrounding tissues.

Heterozygous Having two different alleles at a given locus on a pair of homologous chromosomes.

Hob A (whole) male ferret.

Hobble A castrated (neutered) hob.

Hoblet A vasectomised hob.

Homoeopathy A branch of medicine in which animals are treated with substances that give the same symptoms as those of the disease.

Homozygous The state of having two identical alleles of a particular gene.

Hormone A chemical messenger to the body's organs.

Hybrid Crossed, or produced by crossbreeding two different species e.g. a domestic ferret and a (true) polecat.

Hybrid vigour Where heterosis (increased fitness) increases the strength of different characteristics in hybrids.

Hypoglycaemia Low blood sugar levels, often causing confusion, light-headedness and irritability.

Hypothermia The rapid, progressive mental and physical collapse caused by the lowering of an animal's body temperature.

Inbreeding The practice of breeding together very closely related ferrets. See also 'line breeding'.

Inbreeding depression The deleterious effects that inbreeding can have on a breeding population.

Incisors The front teeth.

Induced ovulation Where the discharge of the ova from the Graafian follicle is induced by the physical act of mating (coitus). When this occurs, the body assumes it is pregnant.

Inheritance The manner in which certain characteristics are passed from one generation to the next.

Intravenous Within a vein.

Isoerythrolysis An immunogenic disease that affects kits within the first week of life.

Jill A (whole) female ferret.

Jillette A spayed (neutered) jill.

Kennel The place where ferrets are bred. See also 'stud'.

Kindle As a verb – to give birth; as a noun – pregnant i.e. 'in kindle'.

Kindling Giving birth.

Kit As a noun, this is a ferret, of either sex, under 16 weeks of age. As a verb, the term means to give birth.

Kitting The act of a jill giving birth.

Lethal factor An abnormality of the genome that leads to death in the womb.

Life expectancy See 'Longevity'.

Line A 'family' of ferrets, bred for several generations.

Line breeding A moderate form of inbreeding.

Litter The kits produced at one birth.

Lochia A greenish fluid discharged from the jill's vagina about 24 hours after she has given birth.

Longevity Length of life.

Lymph A pale, yellowish fluid that contains lymphocytes.

Lymphocytes Cells used to help provide an animal with immunity from diseases.

Malignant Becomes progressively worse, and results, ultimately, in death.

Mating See 'Coitus'.

Meiosis Cell division by which eggs and sperm are produced.

Microphthalmic Tiny eyes.

Minerals Minute constituents of a ferret's diet, without which the ferret will not have a balanced diet.

Monohybrid inheritance A single attribute acquired via biological heredity from the parents.

Monorchid The term applied to a male who has only one testis descended into his scrotum.

Mucus A slime composed of gland secretions, leukocytes and salts.

Multi-hybrid inheritance Several attributes acquired via biological heredity from the parents.

Muzzle A device for preventing the ferret from biting sometimes called a 'cope'; also the name for the ferret's nose.

Necrosis Refers to the death of living tissues.

Necrotic A term applied to dead tissues.

Neonatal Newly born (usually refers to animals less than four weeks of age).

Neural crest The ridge of bone on the top of a ferret's skull.

Neurological Pertaining to the nervous system.

Neutering The castration of a hob (then known as a hobble) or spaying of a jill (then known as a jillette).

Oestrus The state during which a jill will accept a mating. See also 'Heat'.

Oestrus cycle The sexual cycle of a jill.

Ophthalmoscope An instrument for allowing a vet to see inside a ferret's eyes.

Otoscope An instrument for allowing a vet to see inside a ferret's ears.

Ovary The female gonad that manufactures oestrogens and eggs. The male equivalent are the testes.

Overshot A jaw whose upper incisors overlap those on the bottom of the jaw.

Ovulation The release of eggs into the womb to be fertilised by the hob's sperm.

Ovum An egg; the plural is ova.

Oxytocin A hormone, often given in an injection to help ensure that the uterus contracts down properly, and expels all of its contents after giving birth.

Parasites Animals that live on or in other animals (hosts) in a manner that is detrimental to the host. Includes worms (helminths), fleas, mites, lice and ticks. See also 'Endoparasite' and 'Ectoparasite'.

Parturition Giving birth (see also 'Kitting' and 'Kindling').

Parvovirus A virus from the family parvoviridae.

Pathogen An organism that causes disease in another organism.

Pedigree A (usually) written family history of the individual ferret concerned. In some countries, the ferret has to be registered with the governing body of the ferret fancy in that country, before the term 'pedigree (ferret)' may be used.

Pelage Fur, coat.

Periodontal Relating to the mouth, or more specifically the area around a tooth.

Phenotype The physical appearance of a ferret.

Photoperiod Quite literally, the period of light.

Photoperiodism The dependence on the daytime/night-time (or simply light and dark) ratio of various biological functions.

Polygenic Several genes or a trait whose expression is influenced by more than one gene.

Pregnancy See 'Gestation'.

Progesterone A sex hormone, used for oestrus control in jills and also in the treatment of some skin complaints.

Prognosis The forecast for a condition.

Proteins The basic constituents of all living things, and an essential constituent of a balanced diet, for growth and tissue maintenance.

Punnett square A method of showing the potential offspring from two parents.

Radiography The making of x-ray images.

Recessive A gene that is phenotypically manifest in the homozygous state but is masked in the heterozygote by the presence of a dominant allele. A recessive gene will only show in the animal's phenotype if the animal is homozygous for that gene.

Rehydrating fluid See 'Electrolyte'.

Roughage An old-fashioned term for fibre.

Scats Stools, droppings, faecal material. This is a term used for the droppings of all mustelids.

Scours Diarrhoea.

Season See 'Oestrus'.

Selective breeding The selection of certain animals for breeding in order to influence the traits inherited by the next generation.

Sepsis The presence of sufficient bacteria in the blood to cause illness.

Sex chromosomes The chromosomes responsible for determining the sex of a ferret. Hobs have one X chromosome and one Y. Jills have a pair of X chromosomes. All other chromosomes are known as autosomal.

Sex-linked traits Traits or characteristics of an animal that are linked to the sex genes, e.g. the tortoiseshell colouration in cats.

Sexual dimorphism The differences exhibited between the sexes e.g. the hob always has the capacity to grow larger than the jill.

Sibling Brother or sister; litter mate.

Sire The father of a litter.

Spaying A hysterectomy, i.e. the neutering of a jill by removing her uterus. A neutered jill is known as a jillette.

Split Heterozygous.

Spp The abbreviation for more than one species.

Strain A group of related animals of the same species, each of which bears some resemblance to each other, and capable of producing consistent offspring.

Stud An individual 'kennel', where ferrets are bred. Some clubs allow one to register a stud prefix (name) that is exclusive to the registrant. Also, often used to describe the hob used for breeding purposes.

Stud book The record (not necessarily a book) of all the ferrets in a particular stud or breeding programme.

Substrate Floor covering, usually wood shavings.

Supernumerary teeth Extra teeth, i.e. over and above the normal number. The word comes from *super* meaning above, and *numerary* means number.

Sweats, The See 'Heatstroke'.

Systemic Throughout the body.

Taxonomy The scientific discipline of naming organisms.

226

Testes The male gonad, which manufactures androgens and sperm; the female equivalent are the ovaries.

Testosterone An androgen, and the principle male sex hormone.

Throwback The reappearance of an earlier characteristic.

Topical Pertaining to a specific area.

Trait A genetically inherited feature of an organism. Also known as phenotype or character.

Trauma A wound or injury to the body.

Ultrasound A technique used in veterinary medicine, which uses ultra-high energy to obtain images of the internal parts of an animal.

Undershot A jaw whose lower incisors overlap those on the top jaw.

Vaccination An injection of a mild form of a specific pathogenic (disease-causing) microorganism, which causes the body to form antibodies, thus helping to prevent the treated animal from acquiring a full dose of the specific disease, e.g. canine distemper.

Vasectomy The severing of the hob's vasa deferentia, tubes that carry sperm from the testes to the penis, thus allowing the male to mate without producing offspring. A vasectomised ferret is known as a hoblet.

Virus An infectious agent able to cause disease.

Vitamin deficiency The lack of certain important vitamins; this term is usually used to indicate the result of such a deficiency, rather than the actual lack of the vitamin(s) in question.

Vitamins Organic compounds, essential to the health of a ferret. Although they all have chemical names, they are usually referred to by letters of the alphabet, e.g. A, B, C etc.

Weaning The development of the eating habits of kits when they progress from being dependent upon their mother's milk for food, and are capable of feeding themselves, that is, eating solid food.

Zoonoses (zoonotic disease) Diseases capable of being transmitted from a ferret or other animal to humans, e.g. salmonellosis.

Zygote A fertilised egg.

USEFUL ORGANISATIONS

Although the following were all correct at the time of going to press, contact details do change, especially where the organisation is a voluntary one. In all cases, where a reply is required, always enclose a self-addressed and stamped envelope. The inclusion of an organisation does not imply any standard or the author's approval; neither does the exclusion of any organisations imply any disapproval.

Germany
Erste Interessengemeinschaft Frettchenfreunde Hessen
Friedberger Strasse 98
6368 Bad Vilbel 1

Frettchen Club Berlin
Fuchsienweg 18A
D-1000 Berlin 47

Frettchen und Iltisclub NRW
Wehringhauser Strasse 79
5800 Hagen 1

Frettchen und Marderclub Deutschland
Eifelweg 16
30851 Langenhagen

Frettchen Zuchtverband
Dorf Strasse 26
0-1401 Teschendorf

Frettchenfreunde NRW
In der Grossen Heide 6
44339 Dortmund

Netherlands
Stichting de Fret
Boteronstraat 41
1445 LH Purmerend

Norway
Norsk Tamilder Forening
Kastellvcien 20
1162 Oslo 11

Sweden
Stif Vast/Svenska Tam-Iller Foreningen
Norra Barnsjov 19
437 35 Lindome
This organisation has many local groups, details of which can be
supplied from the above address.

Switzerland
SFFS
Hardtstr. 41
CH-5432 Neuenhof

United Kingdom
British Small Animal Veterinary Association
Kingsley House
Church Lane
Shurdington
Cheltenham
Gloucestershire GL51 5TQ

The East Anglian Ferret Welfare Association
35 Lamborne Gardens
Hornchurch
Essex RM12 4LJ

The Essex Ferret Welfare Society
21 Moreton Road
Shelley
Ongar
Essex CM5 0AP

The Gem Ferret Care Group
24 Arden Road
Furnace Green
Crawley
West Sussex RH10 6HS

The Kent Ferret Welfare Society
5 Eastern Gardens
Willesborough
Ashford
Kent TN24 0HE

The National Data Base of Ferret Friendly Vets
Holestone Gate Road
Holestone Moor
Ashover
Derbyshire S45 0JS
Tel: 0870 220 1608
info@ferret-school.co.uk
www.ferret-school.co.uk
A computer data base of veterinary surgeons, established by the author, detailing vets who have experience or interest in ferrets and their ailments. Addition to the data base is free, and enquiries via e-mail are welcomed and are also free.

The National Ferret School
Holestone Gate Road
Holestone Moor
Ashover
Derbyshire S45 0JS
Tel: 0870 220 1608
info@ferret-school.co.uk
www.ferret-school.co.uk
Formed by the author in 1982, the National Ferret School exists to

help educate people to the ways and needs of ferrets. The School travels the UK giving displays and lectures on all aspects of ferrets and ferreting, and runs a variety of courses. The School also sells a wide range of ferret and ferreting equipment, books, videos and DVDs, and publishes its own information sheets on all aspects of ferrets and ferreting.

The Scottish Ferret Club
37 Tutor Road
Leuchars
St Andrews
Fife KY16 0JW

The South East Ferret Club
Westbury 2
Waterditch Road
Warren Street
Lenham
Kent ME17 2DY

South Yorkshire Ferrets
57 Adkins Road
Sheffield S5 8TF

Universities Federation for Animal Welfare
8 Hamilton Close
South Mimms
Potters Bar
Hertfordshire EN6 3QD

Vincent Wildlife Trust
10 Lovat Lane
London EC3R 8DT
This organisation has carried the most extensive research on the ferret's ancestor, the polecat (*Mustela putorius furo*), and has published reports and information sheets detailing this research.

The Wessex Ferret Club
33 Barlow's Road
Tadley
Basingstoke
Hampshire RG26 6NA

United States
The American Ferret Association
PO Box 3986
Frederick
MD 21705

The American Ferret Veterinary Association
1014 Williamson Street
Madison
WI

The Black-Footed Ferret Fund
c/o Wyoming Game and Fish Department
5400 Bishop Boulevard
Cheyenne
WY 82002
Contact this organisation for information on the progress of the
black-footed ferret breeding and re-introduction project, and also
to make donations to help the work of protecting the ferret's most
endangered relative.

The Ferret Fancier's Club
713 Chautauqua Court
Pittsburgh
PA 15214

Ferret Unity and Registration Organisation (FURO)
PO Box 844
Eton College
North Carolina 27244

Ferret World Inc
6 Water Street
Box 555
Assonet
Massachusetts 02702
Manufacturers and distributors of a wide range of ferret equipment.

The International Ferret Association
PO Box 522
Roanoke
Virginia 24003

Marshall Pet Products
5740 Limekiln Road
Wolcott
New York 14590
The largest breeders of ferrets in the US.

The Miami Ferret Club Inc
19225 SW 93rd Road
Miami
Florida 33157

CODE OF ETHICAL PRACTICE FOR FERRET BREEDING

By definition, anyone who breeds one or more litters of ferrets is a ferret breeder, and it is the moral responsibility of all such breeders to ensure that their actions have a positive effect on the species. With this in mind, the following should give a sturdy framework on which breeders can base their actions. Many clubs, societies and other organisations involved with ferret breeding already have such a code; I hope that those that do not, will adopt an ethical code such as this one, and enforce it amongst members.

The following is a brief code that is based on a common sense and practical approach to ferret breeding.

The Code

Ferret breeders will meet all of the needs – both physical and psychological – of the ferrets in their charge.

Ferret breeders will breed with care, being responsible to limit the number of ferrets produced, and will spend the time required to achieve the best ferrets possible.

Ferret breeders will act responsibly in their efforts to produce ferrets for whatever reasons.

Ferret breeders will strive in each and every breeding to achieve the highest quality possible in every litter, in order to maintain the ferret's characteristics.

Ferret breeders will ensure that their actions do not contravene or infringe any law.

Ferret breeders will ensure that each generation of ferrets is as good as, if not better than, the previous generation.

Ferret breeders will use only physically sound, mature ferrets of stable temperament for breeding.

Ferret breeders will never breed overly timid or aggressive ferrets.

Ferret breeders will never breed to develop any over-exaggerated feature(s).

Ferret breeders will never breed to develop a strain/variety that is known to carry serious deleterious hereditary problems.

Ferret breeders will continue to educate themselves regarding genetic diseases pertinent to ferrets.

Ferret breeders will not over-breed any jill, nor breed from any jill that may be too old to cope with the experience.

Ferret breeders will apply the same high standards to jills that are sent to them for breeding purposes.

Ferret breeders will, wherever appropriate, ensure that each ferret in their care is vaccinated and wormed by, or in consultation with, a veterinary surgeon.

Ferret breeders will ensure that all kits are well handled, on a daily basis, before being placed with their new owners.

Ferret breeders will encourage buyers of pet ferrets to spay/neuter wherever appropriate.

Ferret breeders will be honest about the qualities of the ferrets they are placing, explaining both the good, and the not so good points of the species and each individual animal.

Ferret breeders will endeavour to gain personal knowledge of the temperament and health of every ferret they breed, or to which they breed, in order to gather information on which to base future breeding decisions. This information should be shared fully and honestly with other breeders, and with prospective buyers.

Ferret breeders will sell breeding prospects to knowledgeable, ethical, and experienced persons or be willing to help educate and guide novices. They should at any time accept the return of any ferret that their breeding programme produces.

Ferret breeders will not engage in misleading or untrue advertising.

Ferret breeders will never promote ferrets in a way that will encourage reluctant buyers.

Ferret breeders will not sell to impulse buyers.

Ferret breeders will have reasonable assurance that each person receiving a ferret will provide a home with appropriate shelter, restraint, control and responsible care.

Ferret breeders will remain available to serve as a resource, and give free advice and support for typical problems encountered in raising, training and caring for ferrets.

Ferret breeders will participate in, and/or co-operate with, research studies into heritable defects affecting the ferret.

Ferret rescue shelters will not breed from the ferrets in their care.

BIBLIOGRAPHY

Association of British Wild Animal Keepers (ABWAK) – Management of Canids and Mustelids. Proceedings of the 5th symposium of the Association of British Wild Animal Keepers (ABWAK) (1980)

Birks, J.D.S. and Kitchener, A.C. (Eds) – *The Distribution and Status of the Polecat* Mustela putorius *in Britain in the 1990s*. The Vincent Wildlife Trust (1999)

Birks, Johnny – *Mink*. The Mammal Society (1986)

Blood, D.C. and Studder, Virginia P. (Eds) – *Baillières's Comprehensive Veterinary Dictionary*. Baillière Tindall (1988)

Bourdon, Richard M. – *Understanding Animal Breeding*. Prentice Hall (1997)

Bucket, M. – *Introduction to Livestock Husbandry*. Pergamon Press (1977)

Clark, Tim W. – *Conservation Biology of the Black-Footed Ferret*. Wildlife Preservation Trust International (1989)

Clutton-Brock, Juliet – *A Natural History of Domesticated Animals*. Cambridge University Press and the British Museum (Natural History) (1987)

Cooper, B. and Lane, D.R. (Eds) – *Veterinary Nursing*. Pergamon Press (1994)

Cooper, J.E., Hutchinson, M.F., Jackson O.F. and Maurice, R.J. (Eds) – *Manual of Exotic Pets*. The British Small Animal Veterinary Association (1992)

Corbet, G.B. and Hill, J.E. – *World List of Mammalian Species*. The British Museum (Natural History) (1980)

Corbet, G.B., and Harris S. (Eds) – *The Handbook of British Mammals* (3rd edition). Blackwell Scientific Publications (1991)

Dallas, Sue – *Animal Biology and Care*. Blackwell Science (2000)

Dalton, Clive – *An Introduction to Practical Animal Breeding* (2nd Edition). Collins (1985)

Day, Christopher – *The Homoeopathic Treatment of Small Animals*. The CW Daniel Company Limited (1990)

Everitt, N. – *Ferrets – their Management in Health and Disease*. N. Everitt (1897)

Fiedler, Peggy L. and Jain, Subodh K. – *Conservation Biology*. Chapman and Hall (1992)

Fortunati, Piero – *First Aid for Animals*. Sidgwick & Jackson (1989)

Fox, James G. – *Biology and Diseases of the Ferret* (2nd Edition). Lea & Febiger (1998)

Gordon M.S. – *Zoology*. MacMillan (1976)

Grzimek, B. (Ed) – *Grzimek's Animal Life Encyclopaedia* (Vols 10, 11 and 12). Van Nostrand Reinhold (1972)

Hammond, K., Graser, H.-U. and McDonald, C.A. – *Animal Breeding – The Modern Approach*. Post Graduate Foundation in Veterinary Science, University of Sydney (1992)

Hodson, Anna – *Genetics*. Bloomsbury (1992)

Honacki, J.H. and Kinman, K.E. – *Mammal Species of the World*. Allen Press (1982)

Jurd, Richard D. – *Instant Notes in Animal Biology*. BIOS (1997)

Kerr, Hugo – *'What's Wrong With My Pet?'* Hamlyn (1990)

King, Carolyn – *Weasels and Stoats*. Christopher Helm (1989)

Kleiman, Devra G., Allen, Mary E., Thompson, Katerina V. and Lumpkin, Susan (Eds) – *Wild Mammals in Captivity*. University of Chicago Press (1996)

Lloyd, Maggie – *Ferrets – Health, Husbandry and Diseases*. Blackwell Science (1999)

MacDonald, David – *The Velvet Claw*. BBC Books (1992)

MacDonald, David (Ed) – *The Encyclopaedia of Mammals Volume 1*. Guild (1985)

Mason, I.L. (Ed) – *The Evolution of Domesticated Animals*. Longman (1984)

Matthews, L. Harrison – *The Life of Mammals* (Vols 1 and 2). Weidenfield and Nicolson (1971)

McKay, James – *The Complete Guide to Ferrets*. Swan Hill Press (2002)

McKay, James – *The Ferret & Ferreting Handbook*. The Crowood Press (1989)

Michell, A.R. and Watkins, P.E. – *An Introduction to Veterinary Anatomy and Physiology*. British Small Animal Veterinary Association (1993)

Michell, A.R. – *An Introduction to Veterinary Anatomy and Physiology*. British Small Animal Veterinary Association (1999)

Moody, E. Grant – *Raising Small Animals*. Farming Press (1991)

Morris, Desmond – *The Mammals.* Hodder & Stoughton (1965)

Morton, Chuck and Fox – *Ferrets – A Complete Pet Owner's Manual.* Barron's (1985)

Pardiso, Nowak – *Walker's Mammals of the World.* Johns Hopkins University Press (1991)

Pinney, Chris C. – *The Illustrated Veterinary Guide.* TAB Books (1992)

Pinniger, R.S. (Ed) – *Jones' Animal Nursing.* Pergamon Press (1972)

Porter, Val and Brown, Nicholas – *The Complete Book of Ferrets.* Pelham Books (1985)

Primack, Richard B. – *Essentials of Conservation Biology.* Sinauer Associates Inc. (1993)

Quesenberry, Katherine E. and Carpenter, James W. – *Ferrets, Rabbits and Rodents: Clinical Medicine and Surgery.* W.B. Saunders Company (2003)

Reece, William O. – *Physiology of Domestic Animals.* Lea & Febiger (1991)

Roberts, Mervin F. – *All About Ferrets.* TFH (1977)

Robinson, Roy – *Colour Inheritance in Small Livestock.* Fur & Feather (1978)

Schreiber, A., Wirth, R., Riffel, M. and Van Rompaey, H. – *Weasels, Badgers, Civets and Mongooses and their Relatives.* IUCN (International Union for Conservation of Nature and Natural Resources) (1991)

Seal, Ulysses S., Thorne, E. Tom, Bogan, Michael A. and Anderson, Stanley H. (Eds) – *Conservation Biology and the Black-Footed Ferret.* Yale University Press (1989)

Simpson, Gillian – *Practical Veterinary Nursing* (3rd Edition). British Small Animal Veterinary Association (1991)

Sleeman, Paddy – *Stoats & Weasels, Polecats & Martens.* Whittet Books (1989)

Southern, H.N. – *The Handbook of British Mammals.* The Mammal Society (1979)

Svendsen, P. – *An Introduction to Animal Physiology.* Medical and Technical Publishing Company (1974)

Universities Federation for Animal Welfare (UFAW) (Ed) – *The UFAW Handbook on the Care and Management of Laboratory Animals.* Churchill Livingstone (1976)

West, Geoffrey (Ed) – *Black's Veterinary Dictionary.* A. and C. Black (1988)

Willis, Malcolm B. – *Dalton's Introduction to Practical Animal Breeding* (4th Edition). Blackwell Science (1998)

239

Winstead, Wendy – *Ferrets in Your Home*. TFH (1990)

Winstead, Wendy – *Ferrets*. TFH (1981)

Winter, P.C., Hickey, G.I. and Fletcher, H.L. – *Instant Notes in Genetics*. BIOS (1998)

Wolfensohn, Sarah and Lloyd, Maggie – *Handbook of Laboratory Animal Management and Welfare*. Oxford University Press (1996)

Young, J.Z. – *The Life of Vertebrates*. Oxford University Press (1978)

INDEX